Transnational Organiz

C000175741

With organized crime estimated to generate billions of dollars every year through illegal activities such as money laundering, smuggling of people and goods, extortion, robbery, fraud, and insider trading, authorities are increasingly working together to combat this increasing threat to international security and stability.

In this book former police officer Frank Madsen provides a much needed, short and accessible introduction to transnational organized crime, explaining its history and the key current issues, and clearly examining the economics and practices of crime in the era of globalization.

Key issues discussed include:

- The war on drugs
- Anti-money laundering efforts
- The relationship between organized crime and terrorism
- Development of "Internet-based" criminal activity
- International responses to transnational organized crime.

Illustrated by a series of researched case studies from around the world, *Transnational Organized Crime* is essential reading for all students and researchers in international relations, international law, and criminology.

Frank G. Madsen is a researcher in transnational crime at the University of Cambridge. A former police officer with both the Danish police force and Interpol, his research interests include organized crime, corruption, trafficking in women and children, and environmental crime, in particular deforestation.

Routledge Global Institutions

Edited by Thomas G. Weiss
The CUNY Graduate Center, New York, USA
and Rorden Wilkinson
University of Manchester, UK

About the Series

The "Global Institutions Series" is designed to provide readers with comprehensive, accessible, and informative guides to the history, structure, and activities of key international organizations. Every volume stands on its own as a thorough and insightful treatment of a particular topic, but the series as a whole contributes to a coherent and complementary portrait of the phenomenon of global institutions at the dawn of the millennium.

Books are written by recognized experts, conform to a similar structure, and cover a range of themes and debates common to the series. These areas of shared concern include the general purpose and rationale for organizations, developments over time, membership, structure, decision-making procedures, and key functions. Moreover, current debates are placed in historical perspective alongside informed analysis and critique. Each book also contains an annotated bibliography and guide to electronic information as well as any annexes appropriate to the subject matter at hand.

The volumes currently published include:

34 Transnational Organized Crime (2009)
by Frank G. Madsen (University of Cambridge)

33 The United Nations and Human Rights (2009)
A guide for a new era, 2nd edition
by Julie A. Mertus (American University)

32 The International Organization for Standardization and the Global Economy (2009)
Setting standards
by Craig N. Murphy (Wellesley College) and JoAnne Yates (Massachusetts Institute of Technology)

31 Shaping the Humanitarian World (2009)
by Peter Walker (Tufts University) and Daniel G. Maxwell (Tufts University)

by Chris May (University of the West of England)

7 **The UN Security Council (2006)**
Practice and promise
by Edward C. Luck (Columbia University)

6 **Global Environmental Institutions (2006)**
by Elizabeth R. DeSombre (Wellesley College)

5 **Internal Displacement (2006)**
Conceptualization and its consequences
by Thomas G. Weiss (The CUNY Graduate Center) and
David A. Korn

4 **The UN General Assembly (2005)**
by M.J. Peterson (University of Massachusetts, Amherst)

3 **United Nations Global Conferences (2005)**
by Michael G. Schechter (Michigan State University)

2 **The UN Secretary-General and Secretariat (2005)**
by Leon Gordenker (Princeton University)

1 **The United Nations and Human Rights (2005)**
A guide for a new era
by Julie A. Mertus (American University)

Books currently under contract include:

The Organisation for Economic Co-operation and Development
by Richard Woodward (University of Hull)

Regional Security
The capacity of international organizations
by Rodrigo Tavares (United Nations University)

Global Institutions and the HIV/AIDS Epidemic
Responding to an international crisis
by Franklyn Lisk (University of Warwick)

African Economic Institutions
by Kwame Akonor (Seton Hall University)

Non-Governmental Organizations in Global Politics
by Peter Willetts (City University, London)

by Alan Tomlinson (University of Brighton)

International Law, International Relations, and Global Governance
by Charlotte Ku (University of Illinois, College of Law)

**Preventive Human Rights Strategies in a World of New Threats
and Challenges**
*by Bertrand G. Ramcharan (Geneva Graduate Institute of International
and Development Studies)*

Humanitarianism Contested
*by Michael Barnett (University of Minnesota) and Thomas G. Weiss
(The CUNY Graduate Center)*

Forum on China-Africa Cooperation (FOCAC)
by Ian Taylor (University of St. Andrews)

For further information regarding the series, please contact:

Craig Fowlie, Senior Publisher, Politics & International Studies
Taylor & Francis
2 Park Square, Milton Park, Abingdon
Oxford OX14 4RN, UK

+44 (0)207 842 2057 Tel
+44 (0)207 842 2302 Fax

Craig.Fowlie@tandf.co.uk
www.routledge.com

Transnational Organized Crime

Frank G. Madsen

Routledge
Taylor & Francis Group

LONDON AND NEW YORK

First published 2009
by Routledge
2 Park Square, Milton Park, Abingdon, Oxon OX14 4RN

Simultaneously published in the U.S.A. and Canada
by Routledge
711 Third Avenue, New York, NY 10017

*Routledge is an imprint of the Taylor & Francis Group, an informa
business*

© 2009 Frank G. Madsen

Typeset in Times New Roman
by Taylor & Francis Books

British Library Cataloguing in Publication Data
A catalogue record for this book is available from the British Library

Library of Congress Cataloging in Publication Data
Madsen, Frank G.
Transnational organized crime / Frank G. Madsen.
   p. cm. – (Global institutions)
Includes bibliographical references and index.
   1. Organized crime. 2. Transnational crime. 3. Criminal justice,
Administration of–International cooperation. I. Title.
   HV6252.M33 2009
   364.106–dc22
         2008053672

ISBN13: 978-0-415-46498-7 (hbk)
ISBN13: 978-0-415-46499-4 (pbk)
ISBN13: 978-0-203-87582-7 (ebk)

This book is dedicated to Queens' College, Cambridge

Contents

Illustrations

Figures

Tables

Box

Foreword

The current volume is the thirty-fourth new title—several have already gone into second editions—in a dynamic series on "global institutions." The series strives (and, based on the volumes published to date, succeeds) to provide readers with definitive guides to the most visible aspects of what many of us know as "global governance." Remarkable as it may seem, there exist relatively few books that offer in-depth treatments of prominent global bodies, processes, and associated issues, much less an entire series of concise and complementary volumes. Those that do exist are either out of date, inaccessible to the non-specialist reader, or seek to develop a specialized understanding of particular aspects of an institution or process rather than offer an overall account of its functioning. Similarly, existing books have often been written in highly technical language or have been crafted "in-house" and are notoriously self-serving and narrow.

The advent of electronic media has undoubtedly helped research and teaching by making data and primary documents of international organizations more widely available, but it has also complicated matters. The growing reliance on the Internet and other electronic methods of finding information about key international organizations and processes has served, ironically, to limit the educational and analytical materials to which most readers have ready access—namely, books. Public relations documents, raw data, and loosely refereed web sites do not make for intelligent analysis. Official publications compete with a vast amount of electronically available information, much of which is suspect because of its ideological or self-promoting slant. Paradoxically, a growing range of purportedly independent web sites offering analyses of the activities of particular organizations has emerged, but one inadvertent consequence has been to frustrate access to basic, authoritative, readable, critical, and well-researched texts. The market for such has actually been reduced by the ready availability of varying quality electronic materials.

For those of us who teach, research, and practice in the area, such limited access to information has been particularly frustrating. We were delighted when Routledge saw the value of a series that bucks this trend and provides key reference points to the most significant global institutions and issues. They are betting that serious students and professionals will want serious analyses. We have assembled a first-rate line-up of authors to address that market. Our intention, then, is to provide one-stop shopping for all readers—students (both undergraduate and postgraduate), negotiators, diplomats, practitioners from nongovernmental and intergovernmental organizations, and interested parties alike—seeking information about the most prominent institutional aspects of global governance.

Transnational organized crime

Bodyguards to protect public officials and private corporate executives, disappearances, prostitution rings, children in human sexual bondage, and independent drug lords with kingdoms in the jungles are all part of this week's headlines or newscasts. Transnational organized crime is increasingly seen as a threat to international security and stability as well as domestic and global economies. This fundamental concern to national and international decision makers has only recently come to be subject matter for international relations scholars and international lawyers. For some time, police and intelligence practitioners have pointed to the connection between transnational organized crime and state fragility, armed conflict, and terrorism. They have highlighted the complex and problematic relationships between trafficking in arms, human beings, and drugs, and corruption and state failure. These are all topics that figure in many books in the series but most especially in two on money laundering and international criminal pursuit.[1]

We were fortunate to persuade a life-long practitioner recently turned scholar, Frank Madsen of Cambridge University, to write this volume on transnational organized crime for this series. It is a formidable research-based, critical assessment of the subject. He examines and tackles such questions as the use of the "expatriate US dollar," the unending war on drugs, and anti–money laundering efforts. He also scrutinizes the postulated relationship between organized crime and terrorism and introduces the notion of "deviant knowledge," which he applies not only to members of the professions, who place their knowledge at the disposal of criminals, but also to public officials' deviation of knowledge for allegedly superior political reasons.

Frank Madsen has extensive international law enforcement experience—having been both liaison officer and head of criminal intelligence at Interpol's General Secretariat in France, where he wrote *Encyclopaedia* (a restricted circulation handbook on the tracing and forfeiture of criminal assets, which was used by police and customs services throughout the world). During his tenure at Interpol's headquarters, he was involved in the resolution of some of the largest drug cases of that time. His operational field experience, for example in organized crime and financing of terrorism cases, is easily discernable in this book. His two-decade-long experience as director of international corporate security for a US Fortune-100 company afforded him unique practical insights, in particular into industrial espionage, corruption, and fraud, as well as in regards to the analysis of terrorism from a corporate perspective. During this period he also conceived and designed a new industry-wide institute, the Pharmaceutical Security Institute, now located in Washington, DC, with the purpose of monitoring and interdicting the production and sale of counterfeit pharmaceuticals throughout the world.

Having submitted his Ph.D. thesis, on which the present volume is based, to the University of Cambridge in the United Kingdom, he is now a researcher at St. Edmund's College, Cambridge University, where he continues to research transnational organized crime, specializing in the relationship between crime and international relations and governance. He is the author of a chapter on organized crime in *The Oxford Handbook of the United Nations*[2] and of an original paper offering a theory on the scholarly and practical use of scaling and complexity theory in the study of organized crime and terrorism, which is the object of wide interest.[3] Recently he co-wrote an article on energy security for the journal *Gnosis* of the Italian intelligence services.[4] His is a truly original voice in this business.

As always, we look forward to comments from first-time or veteran readers of the Global Institutions series.

Thomas G. Weiss, The CUNY Graduate Center, New York, USA
Rorden Wilkinson, University of Manchester, UK
April 2009

Acknowledgements

First and foremost, I would like to thank the editors of the Routledge Global Institutions series, professors Thomas G. Weiss and Rorden Wilkinson, for having invited me to write this volume in the series and for their helpful comments, recommendations, and corrections during the editing phase.

Second, my appreciation goes to Professor Arthur Gibson for sharing his philosophical insights and for helping me refine my stylistic sensibility. To Police Major General Krerkphong Pukprayura of the Royal Thai Police for guidance and, more importantly, for almost 30 years of friendship. My debt to Scott Ritter of the U.S. Homeland Security Department and to Detective Scott Campbell of Fort Worth Police Department is obvious for a thorough initiation into the intricacies of organized retail and fencing crime. Also, I owe a lot to Messrs. Jonathan I. Polk and Jeffrey B. Pruiksma of the Federal Reserve Bank of New York for their time and patience. I am indebted to Denise Steward of Westlaw for teaching me the use of Westlaw's online services and for permitting me to use the Westlaw Online Law School facility during an academic year spent at Georgetown University Law Center. I thank my friend and former colleague, Mr. D'Arcy Quinn, Counsel, Counterfeit Enforcement, Philip Morris International Tobacco Company, Lausanne, Switzerland, for both general and specific information pertaining to the section "Illicit Traffic in Licit Product" as well as for numerous references to sources.

And finally, I cannot express the profound gratitude I feel to my wife, Bernadette Surya, for providing insights into Arabic and for putting up with me during my rather difficult life transition from corporate America to Cambridge academia.

The "errors and omissions" (to paraphrase the IMF) in the following text are quite obviously due to me; furthermore, some of these very helpful colleagues would most certainly disagree with some of my conclusions, in particular regarding the U.S. money supply and money laundering.

List of Abbreviations

Note: "Dollar" and "$" mean "U.S. dollar," unless indicated otherwise. "Billion" and "trillion" mean, respectively, one thousand millions (10^9) and one million millions (10^{12}), while "tons" refers to metric tons. Unless stated to the contrary, "or" is used as the inclusive disjunction.

AML	Anti-Money Laundering
AMLO	Anti Money Laundering Office (Thailand)
APG	Asia/Pacific Group on Money Laundering
ATM	Automated Teller Machine
BAT	British American Tobacco
BKA	Bundeskriminalamt, the German federal police organization
CATOC	Convention Against Transnational Organized Crime (UN)
CD	Compact Disc
CDD	Customer Due Diligence
CFATF	Caribbean Financial Action Task Force on Money Laundering
CMIR	Reports of International Transportation of Currency and Other Monetary Instruments (U.S.)
CND	Commission on Narcotic Drugs (UN)
CNP	Card Not Present (credit or debit card transaction)
CSEC	Commercial Sexual Exploitation of Children
CTF	Combating Terrorist Funding
DEA	Drug Enforcement Administration (U.S.)
DIA	Direzione Investigativa Anti-Mafia, Italy, created by Law 410 of 30 December 1991. It is an investigative law enforcement structure consisting of personnel from the three major Italian law enforcement organizations, which specializes in the investigation of cases involving organized crime.

ECOSOC	United Nations Economic and Social Council
EAG	Eurasian Group on Combating Money Laundering and Financing of Terrorism
EIA	Environmental Investigation Agency
ESAAMLG	Eastern and Southern Africa Anti-Money Laundering Group
EU	European Union
FARC	Revolutionary Armed Forces of Colombia
FATF	Financial Action Task Force
FBI	Federal Bureau of Investigation (U.S.)
FISA	Foreign Intelligence Surveillance Act (U.S.)
FIU	Financial Intelligence Unit
FRCO	Federal Reserve Cash Office (U.S.)
FRG	Federal Republic of Germany
FY	Financial Year
GAFISUD	Financial Action Task Force of South America
GCP	Gross Criminal Product
GDP	Gross Domestic Product
GIA	Armed Islamic Group (Algeria)
GSPC	Salafist Group for Preaching and Combat (Algeria)
HSBC	Hong Kong and Shanghai Banking Corporation. International bank incorporated in the United Kingdom
ICAP	International Currency Awareness Program (U.S.)
ICPC	International Criminal Police Commission
ICPO	International Criminal Police Organization
INCB	International Narcotics Control Board (UN)
IPC	Intellectual Property Crime
IRA	Irish Republican Army
JIT	Just in Time
LTTE	Liberation Tigers of Tamil Eelam (Sri Lanka)
MENAFATF	Middle East and North Africa Financial Task Force
NCB	National Central Bureau (Interpol)
NCCT	Non-cooperative countries and territories
NCIS	National Criminal Intelligence Service (U.K.)
NGO	Non-Governmental Organization
OECD	Organisation for Economic Co-operation and Development
OLAF	European Anti-Fraud Office (EU)
ONCB	Office of the Narcotics Control Board (Thailand)
OTC	Over the Counter. Pharmaceuticals for which a doctor's prescription is not required
PFLP	Popular Front for the Liberation of Palestine
PIN	Personal Identification Number

PKK	Kurdistan Workers' Party
PRC	People's Republic of China
RICO	Racketeer Influenced and Criminal Organizations Statute (U.S.)
SAR	Suspicious Activity Report (an AML measure)
SEC	Securities and Exchange Commission
TNE	Transnational Enterprise
UNCJIN	United Nations Criminal Justice Information Network
UNDCP	United Nations International Drug Control Programme
UNICEF	United Nations Children's Fund
UNODC	United Nations Office on Drugs and Crime
USB	Universal Serial Bus (IT)
WCO	World Customs Organization
WDR	World Drug Report (UNODC)
WGDP	World Gross Domestic Product
WHO	World Health Organization
WIC	Women, Infants and Children Program, administered by the U.S. Food and Nutrition Service, serves to safeguard the health of low-income women, infants and children up to the age of 5.

Introduction

"Transnational organized crime" is not an institution in the generally accepted senses of this term; the inclusion of a book on that subject in a series called "Global Institutions" could therefore be seen as an abnormality. There are, however, two main reasons to justify the inclusion of this subject in the series. First, transnational organized crime has been seen to mirror the structural characteristics of the licit economy and to exploit the structures thus made available to facilitate and increase international trading activities. Therefore, transnational organized crime is by now seen as an international issue, which must be tackled at the international level.

Second, I have, elsewhere,[1] introduced the notions of complexity and scaling theory into the field of organized crime studies. Using such methodology, the behavior under study can, and should, be seen from two different points of view, while maintaining that it is not possible to have a satisfactory concurrent perception of both aspects. From the viewpoint of very near, the individual, local crime, and from the perspective of the very far, the global movements of goods, people, and monetary instruments are observable. When applying the latter aspect of observation, namely from very far, I argue that the transnational net spun by what—in a kind of shorthand notation—is called "organized crime" constitutes a dynamic horizontal institution, whereby goods, people, services, and monetary instruments meet and satisfy the demand emerging from our many desires. As the influential American essayist Walter Lippmann famously stated of U.S. society, "The high level of lawlessness is maintained by the fact that Americans desire so many things which they also desire to prohibit."[2] The commercial structure that provides the many things we—and not only Americans—both desire, and desire to prohibit, is called *organized crime*.[3] Although it is a strong contention of this work that "organized crime" does not exist as a global institution (that is to say as one organization with global reach and global representation), yet the dynamic network spun around the globe by the various criminal activities considered in this work, does constitute a global institution, albeit one that has no visible constitution or fixed structure. It is constantly changing, while it exhibits a permanent configuration in a dynamic and almost virtual and protean way.

It is an obvious tautology to state that in a legal sense only acts which are criminalized are crimes. It is crucial, however, to comprehend, as Peter Andreas[4] points out, that a century ago, most of the crimes now related to smuggling were at most revenue violations (drugs, endangered species, etc.), which have been criminalized by the expansion of so-called prohibitionist laws. The problem of enforcing such laws has, quite obviously, been exacerbated by the sharply expanding legal international trade, which governments encourage while concurrently attempting to interdict the illegal part. The prime example, of course, is the Prohibition period in the United States, which epitomized the concept known by the term *criminogenesis*. Critiquing this concept will be an important thread throughout the work: When a government or, indeed, the UN Security Council, introduces restrictions on a product or service, which is in demand, that demand will be met, in particular by organized crime.

It is necessary to stress an important conceptual difference between this work and similar works: It will be stressed throughout this work that a top-down view of the phenomenon of transnational crime is less helpful than a bottom-up evaluation. It is difficult, but necessary to comprehend that so-called "crime syndicates" as well as terrorist organizations are funded, in the end analysis, by such apparently less important offences as organized retail theft, coupon fraud, street sale of counterfeit luxury products, and cigarette smuggling; indeed, it is the 50-dollar bag of narcotics sold on the streets of New York and the 20-pound "Gucci" bag in Manchester that provide income to organized crime and determine its structure. Therefore, a number of case studies have been introduced in order to show the bottom-up approach; as far as possible these have been chosen from different parts of the world to avoid distortion by country- or regional specificity.

The remaining part of the Introduction will review how the chapters in the book examine the subject. As noted above, transnational organized crime can be viewed as an informal institution with a permanent, albeit dynamic and invisible constitution. This view subtends the structure of the book, which in six chapters analyzes the structure and development of transnational organized crime and, in the seventh, presents an overview of critical issues and future trends.

Chapter 1 questions the taxonomy of organized crime and the relationship between transnational organized crime and international, "transnational," and municipal law. It also introduces the concept of *societal alienation* as an explanatory element in the social fabric of organized criminals and, most certainly, of corporate criminals.

The following Chapter 2 treats the historical development of the conceptual subject generally referred to as organized crime, including the managerial aspects of organized crime on international level, and it further elaborates the concept of *criminogenesis*, which is a core concept for the understanding of transnational organized crime.

Chapter 3 examines some of the more common transnational crimes, in particular illicit traffic in illicit product and illicit traffic in licit product, before considering the important issue of the implantation of one organized crime organization within the territorial entity of another. The chapter finishes with an important case study, "Operation Green Quest." The study deals with a major case of organized retail crime, which had, and presumably still has obvious relations to international terrorism and therefore provides a suitable introduction to the following chapter.

Chapter 4, in fact, questions the relationship postulated by parts of scholarship and officialdom, alike, between organized crime and terrorism. This interrelationship has attracted wide attention since the terrorist attacks in New York, London, and Madrid at the beginning of the twenty-first century. The chapter, however, introduces the concept of *deviant knowledge* as a crucial element and as a means to a better understanding of the political agitations that subtend the triangular tension between organized crime, terrorism, and the government.

From the beginning of the early 1960s, the study of the economics of crime has developed into an exciting and fruitful academic discipline, outlined in Chapter 5, which also examines the role of the so-called *expatriate dollar*, a term coined to designate U.S. dollar notes circulating outside the United States. This chapter considers the importance of such monetary flow at some length.

Chapter 6 proposes an overview of the international counter-measures against organized crime under two headings, institutions and legislation. It reviews the history and function of international law enforcement cooperation with special regard to the efforts of international organizations, such as Interpol and the United Nations, and critically examines so-called anti-money laundering efforts. To illustrate the latter, the case of the implementation of anti-money laundering statutes in Thailand is considered.

Finally, Chapter 7 presents some critical issues in contemporary debate and praxis before introducing a somewhat pessimistic thread by speculating on the likely crimes, which, in the future, will provide transnational organized crime with its income stream. It thereby reflects on the present author's belief—supported by the book's evidence and analysis—that crime and organized crime will remain with us forever as a significant problem. Nevertheless, the question remains whether such crime will achieve such proportions as in effect influencing the world economy and the relationship between countries.

An Annex provides—in a number of tables—quantitative information, which although not exhaustive, is necessary for a better understanding of the subject matter. Likewise, an Annotated Bibliography points to essential, further reading and to a selection of relatively recent cinematographic creations that, albeit in fictionalized form, nevertheless visually depict actual aspects of transnational organized crime.

Throughout the book, a number of case studies serve not only to elucidate the conceptual development but also, and most importantly, to demonstrate to the reader the reality of transnational crime and to leave him or her with a real, almost hands-on, appreciation of the investigative, prosecutorial, and judicial difficulties that such crimes represent. If the book succeeds, even in a modest measure, in conveying a balanced appreciation of the subject matter, avoiding both sensationalism and blasé minimization, it will have served its purpose.

1 Taxonomy

This chapter isolates the concept of transnational organized crime and examines it in relation to international and municipal law and international criminal law, while attempting to untangle the unstable terminology presently used. Initially, however, the issue of criminology in relation to the so-called *transnational condition* will be considered.[1] The point here is that over the last two centuries criminology as part of social sciences has developed a theoretical foundation for the understanding of crime and society. In view of the transnational nature of the criminality considered in this work, one is led to ask if this theoretical foundation retains its meaning also in this relatively new context.

Criminology and the transnational condition

The traditional discipline of International Relations theory is based on the primacy of the nation-state, which led to an emphasis on the study of power on the one hand and, on the other, political theory and law, in particular international law, in order to establish a law-based system for the peaceful management of interstate affairs.

This dichotomy was somewhat disturbed by the perceived nature of so-called globalization, which seemed to introduce a set of new players on the world scene, while observing an alleged concomitant downsizing of the role of the state.[2] The newcomers included in particular transnational corporations, non-governmental organizations (NGOs), and a class of international rich individuals; these three classes have a certain cosmopolitanism in common, since they are not bound or indeed loyal to any territorially determined entity, and, in other words, they represent a new and different way of constructing individual and collective identities.

Crime definition and crime control have always been at the core of the very notion of sovereignty, so considering that governance has, at least in part, been replaced by global governance, it becomes unavoidable to examine the same issue, crime definition and control, in a global context. In doing so, we are in reality building on the work of the French philosopher Emile Durkheim, who noted that crime is a "normal social fact" and that definition and enforcement of anti-crime measures form an important part of the creation of social order, as well as on the insights of Charles Tilly.[3]

In fact, Durkheim's views are not that surprising; after all, what is a society if not a delimitation of what is and is not acceptable if the identity of that individual society is to be retained. Therefore to say that sovereignty is linked to criminalization, which is a determination of the—obviously non-geographical—borders of society, is, at least to some degree, a tautology. Nevertheless, Durkheim's proposition obviously leads to questions about crime definition and control in a "world social order:" Whose views should be applied and how? Some scholars decry what is a fact, namely that modern states are increasingly incapable of governing transnational crime; this, however, should not come as a surprise considering that the same states were never capable of governing national crime, either. Others, in particular of the so-called critical criminology school, would recommend the study of international flows and complexity in a context other than that of the nation-state in what they term *the sociology behind societies.*[4]

Nevertheless, it remains my opinion that for the foreseeable future the system of nation-states and the various international organizations they have created, and, mostly so, the United Nations and its sister organizations, the World Bank and the International Monetary Fund (IMF), will provide the best and, indeed, the only credible framework for analyzing crime control on global level.

A few, relatively recent phenomena deserve to be emphasized at this point, since their "international" character makes them difficult to comprehend at nation-state level. The most important of these has been referred to above, namely what was termed the newcomers on the international scene. In particular one set of these, the cosmopolitan elite, is of import in this context, not only as such, but also because they have created a new urban entity, the *global city.* Hitherto, the term "global city" has been used to refer to mega-cities, where the urban population was larger than the totality of the rural population in the country. Now, however, this term takes on a new meaning with the creation of a virtual global city, *NyLon,* an amalgamation of New York and London. Indeed, a certain class in each city undoubtedly feels closer to their counterparts in the other city than they do to the inhabitants of their own. Therefore, they travel to and from the two cities, London and New York, and have residences and professional activities in both, thereby creating the new, virtual city. Dubai is also considered a global city in this sense.[5]

As part of this futuristic development, one unfortunately also sees the development of more and more "gated communities" around the world and, partially linked to this concept, the surprisingly important increase in the number of private police when compared with public police personnel. Although walls, virtual and physical, have always been constructed by the elites to keep out the non-elites—one only needs to read a couple of novels from Victorian England to see this—the novelty, I would argue, is the total alienation of a large proportion of the economic elites. In Victorian England, the elites at least came in contact with the non-elites in the form of servants. That this is no longer the case is expressed in the justly famous phrase from a Tom Wolfe novel, "Christ, who were these people?" uttered by a yuppie, when he, exceptionally and involuntarily, came into contact with the non-elites in an airport.[6]

This has a direct bearing on the subject-matter, since this attitude is based on a marginalization, which is neither a result of nor a cause for constrained opportunities. It is *societal alienation*, which, I would argue, also assists in the analysis of—often transnational—corporate crime, if one examines the distance (status, benefits, symbols) between the corporate executive and the average citizen. The subsequent societal alienation on the part of the executive makes it difficult for him or her to understand that the law, enacted by "the others," should apply also to them. It should be noted that my use of *societal alienation* differs somewhat from the common acceptation. For instance, Geyer identifies the fact that societal alienation is not identical to or a subform of interpersonal alienation.[7] On my view, however, his use of the term (societal alienation) is too narrow, since he only or mostly applies it to macro-social structures, institutions, and processes, whereas it quite clearly is also applicable to the social isolation of a group of professionals from other segments of the population, culturally, economically, and, indeed, physically.

International, "transnational," and municipal law

Although transnational crime has been with us for a long time—and presumably for as long as human societies (in the plural) have existed, for example in the form of smuggling, cross-border fraud and trading in illicit goods—the concept of transnational crime, as opposed to a thematic treatment of transnational crimes, such as slave trading, is relatively recent. Unfortunately, the terminology in this field is highly unstable and at least four terms sometimes overlap each other, often are synonyms, and occasionally delimit different, albeit related areas: namely "transnational crime,"[8] "transnational organized crime,"[9] "international organized crime,"[10] and "multinational crime."[11]

As an illustration of the terminological instability in this area, it is instructive to observe that in United Nations Security Council resolution 1373 of 2001, §4, the Security Council "*Notes* with concern the close connection between international terrorism and transnational organized crime ... " Terrorism, in other words, is seen by the UN Security Council as *international* while organized crime is *transnational*.[12]

Apart from the purely terminological issue, a more substantial difficulty is the conceptual collocation of the subject-matter in the context of international law; this can best be illustrated by the use of a Venn diagram, which allows a visual understanding of the conceptual difficulties (Figure 1.1).

Among the intersections of the three circles in this diagram, four are of particular relevance to this area of study (∩ is the intersection symbol (elements of sets overlap) and "–" is the complement symbol (elements not in the set)):

1 (IL ∩ TC) ∩ –OC: Crimes that are transnational and a violation of international law, yet not part of organized crime, for example a parental dispute over custody of a child, where one parent "snatches" the child in one country and transfers it to another.

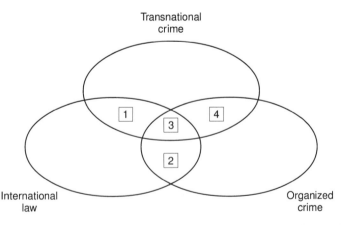

Figure 1.1 Venn diagram. Transnational crime, organized crime, and international law
Note: TC = Transnational Crime; OC = Organized Crime; IL = International Law
Source: Present author

2 (IL ∩ OC) ∩ –TC: Crimes that are organized and a violation of international law, but which do not cross borders, such as slave trading within a country; organized crime's involvement in modern slavery (violation of *ius cogens*, but not necessarily transnational).[13]

3 (IL ∩ TC ∩ OC): Crimes that are transnational, organized, and a violation of international law, for instance international drug trafficking.

4 (TC ∩ OC) ∩ –IL: Crimes that are organized and transnational, but not violations of international law, for example the smuggling of genuine, but non-taxed tobacco product from one country to another.

Transnational crimes are crimes that in one of several ways involve two or more sovereign jurisdictions, but which are codified in the national legislations of these jurisdictions. On the other hand, it is important to emphasize that "transnational crime" is not a synonym for "international crime" as criminalized in international criminal law; a transnational crime may be criminalized under international criminal law, for example drug trafficking, which is the subject of several international conventions and therefore of international law; it does not have to be, though. Another, surprising difference is that a violation of international criminal law does not need to involve more than one country, whereas a transnational crime must.

Transnational crime and international criminal law

Today, the term *transnational organized crime* is commonly used to describe the international cooperation and in general the international aspects of organized crime. At this point it is useful to consider the terminological question from a typical range of current socio-political and psycholinguistic points of view, since it has been questioned by a number of scholars. The objections most often marshaled against the term *transnational organized crime* are of three orders: (i) what the term says, the *denotative meaning*; (ii) what the term does not say but implies, the *connotative meaning*; and (iii) what the term excludes (the *socio-political exclusionary meaning*).[14] Scholars object to the term because the nucleus of it, *organized crime*, is in itself a term that gives rise to much discussion and which is not defined in the criminal codes of a number of jurisdictions.[15] To increase the confusion, according to these critics, the adjective *transnational* is then added without a proper explanation of the difference, if any, between it and *international*. Furthermore, on the second point scholars maintain that the term *transnational organized crime* carries the connotation of "foreign" and as such is xenophobic and racist, notwithstanding the fact that the vast majority of organized criminals are indigenous to the country in which they operate. Finally, the same scholars object that the term excludes crimes such as corporate crime, white-collar crime and in general crimes committed by "the powerful," as expressed by James Sheptycki:

> That is why some concepts articulated within the discourse, those to do with financial crime, economic crime, white-collar crime, crimes of the powerful, serious fraud in the private sector, corporate crime and corruption, environmental crime, war crimes, and state crime are only heard *sotto voce.*[16]

However, Sheptycki's argument that white-collar and corporate crime are excluded from the definition of organized crimes could perhaps be countered in two ways: first, the use in white-collar and corporate crimes of the Racketeer Influenced and Criminal Organizations statute (RICO), the organized crime provision par excellence in the United States; and, second, the sentencing levels in corporate crimes, which would appear to be on the same level as sentencing in organized crime cases—or, indeed, higher. In fact, although RICO was enacted in the United States to counter "the infiltration of organized crime and racketeering into legitimate organizations operated in interstate commerce,"[17] instead prosecutors have relied on the Act to "strike at those—whether or not they fit the ordinary definition of 'racketeerer' or 'organized criminal'—who commit crimes in conducting the affairs of business, labor unions, and government offices."[18]

One of the earliest writers in the field, André Bossard,[19] informally "defined" transnational crimes as those whose resolution necessitates the cooperation between two or more countries: (i) because the crime itself is transnational in so far as it implies crossing at least one border before, during, or after the fact, such as international drug trafficking; (ii) by the consequences; an example is currency counterfeiting in one country, but introduction of the counterfeit notes in the financial system of another; (iii) by the transnational character of the crime; a rather typical case is constituted by gangs of highly professional pickpockets, who ply their trade for a couple of days in one country and then move on to another before law enforcement authorities realize that an organized crime is in execution.[20] Bossard notes that the constitutive elements of transnational crime are two: first, the crossing of a border by people (the criminal), objects (for example firearms), or even the intent or will as in computer fraud, when a cyber criminal gives an order from one country, which is transmitted to and executed in another country; and, second, the "international" recognition of a crime, through international conventions, extradition treaties, or concordant national laws.[21] Bossard's views are obviously influenced by his having served for many years as a high-ranking official at the General Secretariat of Interpol, then in Saint Cloud, France, and he is, quite understandably, pragmatic, having observed the difficulties in transborder law enforcement cooperation.[22] Nevertheless, his insistence on the definitional aspect of *cooperation* is stimulating and fruitful compared to a more legalistic approach. After all, it is fairly clear that the difficulties inherent in the subject-matter which Bossard treats, transnational crime, are not necessarily of a legal nature, but are linked to the issue of cooperation and thus—in the ultimate analysis—to political will. Peter Andreas and Ethan Nadelmann's characterization of transnational crime is, on the other hand, difficult to understand: "We define transnational crime as those activities involving the crossing of national borders and violation of at least one country's criminal laws."[23] The problem here obviously is that they posit transnational crime as the violation of *one* country's criminal laws. If the activity in question only violates one country's criminal law and in other words there are no concordant national laws, then, with a few treaty-based exceptions, there will be no international law enforcement cooperation, no extradition, etc. It is difficult to comprehend the contents of the term "transnational crime" on this view.

Finally, it should be noted that the legislator has codified the term *transnational crime* in some jurisdictions. An example is the United States, where Pub. L. 106–386, October 28, 2000, SEC.102.b.24 states that: "Trafficking in persons is a *transnational crime* with national implications."[24]

Having considered the taxonomical difficulties implied by the term "transnational organized crime" and its relationship with international law in this chapter, the next two chapters will examine, respectively, its history and development (Chapter 2) and its factual contents (Chapter 3).

2 History and development of the concept of organized crime

This chapter will consider the formulation and development of the concept of "organized crime," the definitional difficulties identified by scholarship, and the inability of present conceptualizations satisfactorily to account for transnational crime and crime organizations in an age of globalization. The perceptual outcome of this inability which obtains today is to view organized crime as a closed ethnic group.[1]

A further issue, which renders conceptualization difficult, is the increasing co-mingling of illicit and licit businesses run by organized crime groups. Also the illicit trade in licit product such as untaxed cigarettes by organized crime deepens the conceptual complexity. Finally, one must question the dividing line between organized crime and so-called white-collar crime, another criminological conceptualization, which sits awkwardly with criminal justice studies. French scholars have asked the above question and have pointed out that it is perhaps not possible to establish a dividing line between the two kinds of criminality—apart from the rather amusing fact that white-collar crime relies on an illegal back room and organized crime on a legal front room.[2]

As noted in the introduction, *criminogenesis* forms an important thread throughout the work. Over the last century, two concurrent developments are of import in the present context: first, that a number of acts, such as the trafficking in arms and narcotic drugs, have been criminalized, creating a *prohibition regime*; and second, that a number of such prohibition regimes have homogenized and converged into an *international prohibition regime*, under pressure from governments and so-called transnational moral entrepreneurs, exemplified by NGOs.[3] It is not within the scope of the present work to consider the motivations behind such governmental and non-governmental criminalizing efforts. Nevertheless, the following points need to be made:

(i) Basically all criminalization by bi- or multilateral agreements or international prohibition regimes is the promotion and international codification of norms generated in the Occident and in particular in the United States.

(ii) NGOs and other transnational moral entrepreneurs promote and export norm sets based on ethical considerations without clarifying whose ethics they are promoting and without explicating why that particular set of norms is superior to other sets of norms and deserves to be internationally accepted.

The concept of organized crime

The concept of *organized crime* was born in the United States in the nineteenth century; nevertheless, there has been little agreement throughout history as to the contents of the concept. The two criminologists, Goldthaite Dorr and Sidney Simpson,[4] claimed in their 1929 publication that organized crime consists in two activities, *criminal fraud* and *the protection racket*, thus concentrating on the behavioral aspect of organized crime instead of on racial and ethnic aspects. Unfortunately, the U.S. government, and a large part of scholarship, did not follow this advice, but concentrated on a perceived collective identity rather than on behavioral characteristics. There seems to be little doubt that such an approach by the U.S. government was much influenced by the then-recent St. Valentine's Day Massacre in 1929 in Chicago, in the course of which a crime group of Italian origin, under the leadership of the later rather notorious criminal Al Capone, killed seven members of a rival group of Irish origin in what appeared to be an execution; this event quite understandably caused a public outcry.[5] The perceptual outcome was based on a view of organized crime as a closed ethnic group, often of Italian origin, based on tribal or family relationships, etc. The choice of relying on the so-called "Sicilian syndrome" or the "alien conspiracy" model has gravely impeded scholarship in relevant conceptualization of the subject-matter.[6] The Sicilian syndrome is based on important studies of Sicilian organized crime over the last 150 years[7] and was used as a model for the bulk of subsequent studies elsewhere in the world. This choice, however, was also based on political expediency, since, politically, it was preferable to apprehend the phenomenon as a conspiracy of foreigners against a basically sound domestic society. Nevertheless, it is by now clear that the Sicilian model cannot be exported and evident that it does not fit organized crime in other times and other countries with different societal problems and policies. It is equally obvious that organized crime is not necessarily imported into the country in which it operates. Rather, it is or can be a symbiotic societal phenomenon, which—furthermore—satisfies demands for illicit goods and services that are generated by the allegedly "sound" domestic society.

The U.S. governmental paradigm, which served as inspiration for the so-called RICO statute, was based on the conclusions of the Ronald Reagan Presidential Commission on Organized Crime of 1983.[8] It continued the overall view of organized crime as a national and international conspiracy; it also formed the conclusion that organized crime has many of the structures of legitimate corporations, in particular an innate wish to obtain market monopoly. The government paradigm had a certain commonality with the alien conspiracy model since it noted the presence of "traditional organized crime" (Italian), but claimed that this was now being threatened by a number of upcoming crime groups of Asian and Latin American origin. It overemphasized the cohesiveness, power, and potential reach of the Mafia and the new groups, when viewed as institutions, and disregarded any interaction with a postulated "sound society."[9]

The officially adopted organized crime paradigm served as a basis for policy determination, but was widely rejected by scholars. In reaction, Stephen Mastrofski and Gary Potter proposed a "flexible network model," which saw organized crime as an informal, loosely structured, open system reactive to fluctuations in the economic, political, and legal environment in a postulated symbiosis between the upperworld[10] and the underworld, making it very difficult to distinguish the corrupter from the corrupted.[11] This and similar conceptual views of organized crime are perhaps the most appropriate ones developed so far and they have gained the approval of an important part of modern scholarship. Whatever one might think about the various paradigmata proposed by scholarship, it is important to keep in mind that overwhelmingly organized crime in general and transnational organized crime in particular is a response to demand, but *denied demand*.

The term *organized crime* is a generalization, which covers a highly complex matter that, as a result, is difficult to define in a significant manner, inter alia because to formulate a fully generalized concept, it would have to be stretched to incorporate a whole series of criminal behavioral patterns in a multitude of spatio-temporal relationships. I argue that organized crime is first and foremost a commercial entity. Therefore a comparison with the franchising industry appears more justified, and it provides an interesting way of improving the imagery of organized crime and also allows for a better understanding of *density differential*.

One can compare organized crime with McDonald's restaurant franchises. In rural areas there is a great distance between each such restaurant, in suburbia less, and in city centers, in particular in the United States, there is one every few blocks. Organized crime and gangs follow the same pattern, which explains why the "turf," the jurisdiction, of each gang chief in city centers is exiguous; but it is nevertheless the object of fierce competition as neighboring gangs eye it covetously.[12] A further issue, which renders conceptualization difficult, is the increasing co-mingling of illicit and licit businesses run by organized crime groups.[13] The most authoritative definition of organized crime to date is without doubt the one adopted in the December 2000 UN Convention against Transnational Organized Crime (CATOC), according to which organized crime is a

> structured group of three or more persons, existing for a period of time and acting in concert with the aim of committing one or more serious crimes or offences in order to obtain, directly or indirectly, financial or other material benefit.[14]

The UN Office on Drugs and Crime[15] opined in 2002—perhaps somewhat hastily—that "by providing a standard set of agreed upon definitions … the Convention and its Protocols have in effect established a base-line for future research and analysis." Already, one of the major scholars in the field, Margaret E. Beare,[16] has dismissed the CATOC definition as being "way too broad," just as she, for the same reason, rejected the definition proposed by Sam Porteous[17] in his report to the Solicitor General of Canada, which was adopted by the Canadian government. Porteous identified organized crime as

> economically motivated illicit activity undertaken by any group, association or other body consisting of two or more individuals, whether formally or informally organized, where the negative impact of said activity could be considered significant from an economic, social, violence generation, health, and safety and/or environmental perspective.

In the United States, the Federal Bureau of Investigation (FBI) defines organized crime as

> any group having some manner of a formalized structure and whose primary objective is to obtain money through illegal activities. Such groups maintain their position through the use of actual

or threatened violence, corrupt public officials, graft, or extortion, and generally have a significant impact on the people in their locales, region, or the country as a whole.[18]

A comparison between the Canadian and the U.S. FBI definitions shows first and foremost that in the U.S. case, a group must have a "formalized" structure; in Canada not necessarily. Also, the Canadian definition refers in a more general way to the social damage caused by organized crime, in particular to environmental damage, whereas the American definition underlines the corrupting influence of this form of crime.

Finally, Interpol has since 1988 proposed its own definition of organized crime:

> Any enterprise or group of persons engaged in a continuing illegal activity which has as its primary purpose the generation of profits irrespective of national borders.[19]

Richard Friman and Peter Andreas, on the other hand, turn the question upside-down and ask neither who commits the criminal acts, nor in which such criminalized behavior might consist, but instead where such activities take place. And they furnish the answer themselves:

> The gap between the state's metapolitical authority to pass prohibition laws and its ability to enforce such laws fully is the space where clandestine transnational actors operate.[20]

Models in organized crime

Over the last 30 years, scholarship has attempted to elaborate models—sometimes called paradigms—for the study of organized crime. It is not clear that the use of such models has had any major success in providing a deeper and more nuanced image of organized crime. There are undoubtedly several reasons for this, in particular that it is difficult to model human behavior without making a series of assumptions, which render the very model incomprehensible. Second, and perhaps more importantly, one must realize that although dealing with the subgroup of crime termed "organized crime," the differences between the predatory, opportunistic, traditional methodologies, membership configurations, decisional authority sharing, etc., are so wide that no model can relevantly subtend all of them. If one insists on using models, I would suggest that a biological point of view might be more helpful as an aid to an intellectually satisfactory conceptualization; cells are autonomous, meet in hostile or cooperative situations, and survive, albeit sometimes in a changed form, almost any attempt to destroy them.

The "organized" in organized crime

The question of what exactly constitutes organized crime is far from having been satisfactorily solved on the academic level. Nevertheless, a first approach might be to focus on the term *organized*, that is, not only crime, but crime that has been organized or, maybe even more precisely, crime that has been managed. A number of case studies throughout this book are meant to illustrate the management effort inherent in the execution of even the simplest or simpler criminal acts on the transnational level; for example, Chapter 3 includes studies of, respectively, an international credit card fraud and of Chinese organized crime in Italy. Considering the pure scale of counterfeit products from the People's Republic of China (PRC) available at street level in Italy, which Confesercenti[21] estimates at €7 billion in yearly turnover,[22] one can easily imagine the managerial effort involved in the manufacturing and smuggling phase alone, without even mentioning the highly complex distribution level. It is worth mentioning, en passant, that on the distribution level a considerable number of persons are employed and, as pointed out, inter alia by Donald Liddick, a "disenfranchised population sees organized crime as an opportunity for jobs and as a way to a better life."[23] From the point of view of "citizen safety," though, one notes with concern in the listing of counterfeit products offered for sale by the organization several items that—apart from being illegal for sale—are also extremely dangerous, such as counterfeit motor vehicle and aircraft spare parts. These are inevitably manufactured from sub-standard steel, and the use of such spare parts in the disks of braking systems on high-performance automobiles such as Mercedes and BMW has, in the past, led to fatal accidents. The same holds true for the use of similar spare parts in aircraft.

There are, undoubtedly, many complex explanations for the existence and persistence of organized and, subsequently, transnational organized crime, ranging from socio-economic to socio-psychological ratiocinations. One cannot, however, but point to a justly famous scene in a novel by the Sicilian writer Leonardo Sciascia, in which an old Mafioso speaks to a recent recruit:

"The people were cuckolds and they still are."
"But we, my dear boy, walk on the horns of others, like dancers."[24]

A less elegant U.S. organized crime equivalent is: "Only suckers work."[25] The disdain speaks for itself and I am not persuaded that the economical analysis of crime and, in particular organized crime, is founded on a solid base, since it presupposes that criminals are rational beings, who would choose legal over illegal activities were the profitability equal or superior. In fact, from statements such as the above, as well as from my personal dealings with organized crime, it seems to me more than probable that—on top of obvious rational considerations—there is a psychological element involved in the choice, which is difficult to define precisely. It includes a component of the sheer adrenalin rush from living dangerously, in a sense outside society, and looking at the individuals making up society as inferior, because they live by society's rules, not, according to this thinking, out of choice, but out of fear and weakness since they are not strong enough to create and live by their own. This argument, although definitely not conclusive, is backed up by a consideration of the possible interpretation of the etymology of the names of the three main Italian criminal organizations, which all contain an element of the fact of being able to establish and live by one's own rules.

Mafia, 'ndrangheta, Camorra: *etymology*

To avoid over-reliance on the so-called Sicilian syndrome, this work attempts to draw on experiences from many societies. Nevertheless, it is of import to dwell on the etymology of the names of the three major Italian crime organizations, the Mafia (Sicily), the 'ndrangheta (Calabria), and the Camorra (Campania), as a philological consideration of these leads us to an understanding, not of the structural particularities of organized crime, but of the attitudinal characteristics of its members.

There is no agreement as to the etymology of the term *mafia*; I would tend to agree with Alison Jamieson, who argues that the term seems to originate from tenth-century Arabic, from the time of the colonization of Sicily by the Arabs, when *mahias* meant "impudent, arrogant."[26] It is certainly no coincidence that the second time the term *mafia* is found in written Italian, albeit in its adjective form, it is used of a young woman, who is described as "carusa e mafiusa" (pretty and self-assured).

The term *'ndrangheta* is more obvious, etymologically, being a contraction of the Greek words *andros* and *agathos*, recalling that southern Italy once was Magna Graecia. Originally, "andros agathos" meant a "noble man," a high-born or noble-born man, and then "a courageous or brave man," since courage and bravery were seen as characteristics of high birth. The typical embodiment of the concept of being an "andros agathos," or of being "good or competent" as a man, in Ancient Greece undoubtedly was Ulysses, courageous and good at all aspects of life from wielding a sword to building a house to steering and commanding a ship. This leads to the inner meaning, originally, of the terms *mafia* and *'ndrangheta* as a person, who is self-assured, capable of taking care of his own business without invoking the help of institutions and outsiders, and who will not, since he is "noble and courageous," allow any infringement of his rights.

The term *camorra* (organized crime in the region of Campania in Italy) is not etymologically simple. There are several possible explanations of the origin of this term, of which the most probable is that it originally signified a tax one had to pay in a gambling den to the security personnel, who were present in case of disagreements and fights. The etymology would then be extracted from "ca'" or "capo" (chief, boss) and "murra" or "morra", the then prevalent gambling game (now prohibited) in particular among the poorer parts of the population. In fact, this is the signification of the term in an official document from the Kingdom of Naples in 1735. In other words, a tax paid to a kind of enforcers, who enforced non-official rules and who did not need the assistance in any way of officials in the Kingdom to run and enforce the rules of their businesses.

This parenthesis, dealing with the socio-psychological fabric of the organized criminal to some extent evokes the idea of individuality. Extreme individualism is, however, only present in the individual's dealings with society as such, since organized criminals have developed the ability to integrate themselves into a criminal structure, comprising rules and disciplinary processes in a mimetic recreation of the management culture of society, which is exactly what renders *organized* crime possible.

The management talents of organized crime

In order to analyze the "corporate" elements of transnational crime, two crucial concepts will be introduced in this chapter, *organizational talent* and *speed of execution*. They are both part of organized crime viewed as business and as such linked to the economics of crime, but are treated here since they illustrate the very real managerial capabilities of organized crime in a more meaningful way than recitals of shootings, etc.

As an example of the organizational talents of organized crime, one might consider the seizure on 9 May 2008, in Naples, Italy, of 8 tons of counterfeit Marlboro cigarettes originating in China. The case itself will be further analyzed in Chapter 3, but at this initial stage even a brief consideration reveals the management effort which must have been expended. First, for the actual production of the cigarettes: the operator needs to obtain the tobacco product, the cigarette paper and the filter, all of an appearance and tactile quality which would enable the cigarettes to pass for the genuine brand product. The counterfeiter would also need access to cigarette rolling (producing) machinery, which, again, would need to be of a quality sufficient for a product that would not attract the attention of the smokers, since cigarettes too tightly or too loosely rolled would immediately be noticed by an experienced "one-brand" smoker. Second, on the printing side, the counterfeiter would need to obtain cigarette boxes, cartons, and master cartons of acceptable quality; in the experience of the present author, the printing and packaging might not take place in the same location or, indeed, in the same country as the production. Third, the counterfeiter would need to export the cigarettes or sell them to an exporter in China. In either case, false customs and other export documentation would be required. Fourth, the counterfeiter or the exporter would have to have established contact with an overseas importer, who would have to carry out the importation and thus the customs formalities. The importer would have to have access, directly or indirectly, to a number of individuals, who could distribute the product. There is here a further managerial complication for the criminal organization, since the counterfeit packaging—in order for the tobacco product to be sold at full retail prices—must include the correct, but counterfeit tax sticker showing that the appropriate taxes have been paid in the "end country," in which the retail sale occurs. Finally, the financial engineering would have to be worked out, whereby everybody involved in the chain would be paid and adequate disposal arrangements made for any centrally accrued funds.

The management effort is what is reflected in the "organized" of organized crime. In summary form: highly efficient, intercultural, networked cooperative capabilities comparable to the most efficient modern management techniques. Without being overly philosophical, one might surmise that organized crime in its entrepreneurial aspects in some ways is mimetic of transnational enterprises and their techniques, from global supply lines to jurisdictional arbitrage. Or, as the French examining magistrate Thierry Cretin amusingly points out, we were used to the criminal entrepreneur; now we have to get used to the entrepreneurial criminal.[27] However entrepreneurial, though, the criminal might be in order to manage his or her operations smoothly, he or she must interact with the society in which the criminality in question is embedded and ensure, as far as possible, the cooperation or inaction of the services created to control or interdict such operations. One of the characteristics of organized crime is that its members have developed—some would say "perfected"—the very tools with which to obtain this happy state of affairs: corruption.

Corruption

Most, if not all of the illicit activities treated in this work would be impossible without corruption. To use an analogy from human anatomy, if monetary funds of licit or illicit origin are like the bloodstream, then corruption would be the lymphatic system. Corruption is the lubricant, which allows the various mechanisms to operate smoothly. Corruption is everywhere and often quite small. In aggregate terms, however, corruption payments are considerable and, according to the World Bank, may constitute more than 3 percent of the world economy. Thus, the World Bank found that in the 2001–2 economy, which worldwide was approximately $30 trillion, corruption payments amounted to $1 trillion dollars, not including embezzlement of public funds or theft of public assets.[28]

Unfortunately, as is the case for "organized crime" and for "terrorism," there is little agreement among scholars as to the definition of corruption. The scholar Vito Tanzi, who at the International Monetary Fund studied the shadow economy and in particular corruption, proposes the definition of corruption as being "the intentional non-compliance with the arm's-length principle aimed at deriving some advantage for oneself or for related individuals from this behaviour."[29] The introduction of the *arm's length principle* is important, but it is equally important to understand that this is much easier to implement in countries with little or no tradition of family or kin adhesion, as for example in Scandinavia, than in countries where, traditionally, family and clan have represented the core values in society and where, as a consequence, a conflict between these values and abstract Weberian bureaucratic idealizations inevitably will be resolved to the advantage of the former.

In a thoughtful speech to a world forum on corruption and integrity, the Canadian Secretary of State for Asia-Pacific, David Kilgour, underlined that corruption discourages domestic as well as foreign direct investment, it creates unease among aid donors and, in certain parts of the world, it facilitates the trafficking in narcotic drugs, arms, and humans. Corruption is furthermore often accompanied by violence, coercion, and political and social unrest. And Kilgour noted that the rule of law, transparency, and efficient anti-corruption measures are indispensable for the creation of a vibrant, investment-friendly business environment.[30] Some scholars would not necessarily agree with the latter statement, since two of the more corrupt countries in the world, India and China, exhibit the highest economic growth rates.[31]

It is often very difficult to state with certainty if corruption is taking or has taken place. For instance, in 1988 the U.S. Commerce Department studied the question of sugar quotas and disclosed the following information. The 29 U.S. senators who had received at least $15,000 each from the sugar industry in political sponsorship, all voted for the quotas, while the senators who received nothing, voted against. The Commerce Department calculated the loss to consumers at an estimated $3 billion per year. It is obviously not possible to state with certainty that corruption had taken place although the numbers tell their own story.[32] This exemplifies the observation that corruption payments can be immediate and explicit (bribes) or delayed (generous gifts to daughter's marriage or job offer to son when he completes studies.)[33] While for example the present author in practical work has relied on the rule of thumb that corruption is paying an official for doing what he or she should not do, or not to do what he or she should do, a separate form of corruption, involving third parties, has developed in India. In these cases officials inform potential users of the bureaucracy that they cannot guarantee performance but a bribe will ensure that the competitor will not be allowed to complete the process. In other words, if one's competitor needs and is entitled to a license, one pays the appropriate official for not according it.[34]

Corruption can be documented in the history of humanity over the last several thousand years. Thus, the city-state of Athens enacted severe anti-corruption laws almost 2,500 years ago; the very existence of such laws demonstrates the prevalence of the phenomenon of corruption. This chapter, however, finishes with a case study closer to our time, namely New York around the 1860s, showing how corruption had permeated the institutions and, in a general way, illustrating the various issues discussed above.

Case study: the gangs of New York

The title of this case study is an obvious reference to Martin Scorsese's 2001 movie of the same name. The fictional date of the film is the 1860s and its action is mainly concentrated in the Five Points area of Manhattan, so called from the five-point configuration created by the intersection of Park, Worth, and Baxter Streets, which throughout the nineteenth and the beginning of the twentieth century was an ill-famed slum. The present case study, however, is to a large degree based on Timothy Gilfoyle's important work, *City of Eros.*[35]

This particular case study was chosen for several reasons. First, one wished to show the very interesting and serious background for a popular movie—thereby introducing also the Seventh Art (the cinematographic art) into the discussion. Second, the rise of organized crime in New York already in the nineteenth century had a clearly transnational nature by international trafficking in women. Finally, one of the main characteristics of "Mafia-type organized crime" as opposed to more general "organized crime" is the insidious relationship between such crime and local, regional, or national politics: Although in nascent form, this is well documented for New York in the nineteenth century by the creation and development of so-called machine politics.

Throughout most of the nineteenth century and the beginning of the twentieth century, the sex trade in Manhattan was the main source of income for local crime and it was linked, directly and indirectly, to local politics, and this to such a degree that a local judge in the 1880s described Manhattan as being ruled by a "noctivagous strumpetocracy." Brothel owners were part of local organized crime and not only were often linked to local politicians; indeed, they often were local politicians—and occasionally members of Congress, as for example Big Tim Sullivan.[36] Needless to say, in the circumstances local police could not but be fully corrupted: In 1894, in the most extensive examination of law enforcement in nineteenth-century New York, State Senator Clarence Lenox concluded that prostitution had been and presumably still was "fostered and protected by the police of the city." And in 1896, the then Police Commissioner (and later president of the United States) Theodore Roosevelt admitted that New York's police system was simply a "business of blackmail and protection."[37]

Prostitution was never legalized in New York as it had been for example in Louisiana; nevertheless the New York police and local politicians, the so-called "political machine," developed an elaborate system of maintenance and control over the most prominent institutions of prostitution, whereby brothel owners paid the local precinct commander or the so-called "wardman" (from 1686 to 1938 New York used the term "ward" for its smallest political units.)[38]

Although prostitution in the rougher parts of Manhattan such as Five Points and Hell's Kitchen is best known, prostitution had permeated society, albeit in different forms, depending on the socio-political level of the area.[39] As early as the eighteenth century, the sex trade had a distinctly international character; by the end of the century, young girls were sold to brothels in New York, a practice which is documented from 1793, when Moreau de St. Méry discovered the trade in Philadelphia, where girls were bought from their parents for $30 per girl. By the 1860s, Italian brothel madams had established a system of bringing young children to the United States, allegedly to work as organ grinders, but in reality as prostitutes, and by the beginning of the twentieth century, some employment agencies operated as intermediaries for brothel madams and were sending agents to Europe for the purpose of "collecting girls." The international character of the trade was clear also to observers, and in 1909 the anti-vice crusader Hattie Ross reported that "Almost without exception these men are foreigners"—"these men" being those running the brothels.

An important example of the genesis, functioning, and political ties of organized crime is provided by the syndication of parts of New York's vice industry in the late nineteenth century. It should be emphasized that although one today—through such films as *Gangs of New York*—could get the impression that organized crime and in particular organized crime in New York is a quaint folkloristic issue, the subject of syndication, in a different form and in different areas, subtends the Italian term *transversalità*, whereby is meant the horizontal integration between organized crime decision makers and political decision makers. In the last decades of the nineteenth century, New York's police and the political machine had brought de facto regulation to the prostitution industry in New York as a result of a process—profitable to police officials and politicians as well as to the brothel owners and pimps—that had slowly evolved over the century. The political link, which made it possible to syndicate and more or less openly exploit an illegal activity, prostitution, was Tammany Hall, the New York Democratic Party political machine from 1789 to 1961. Tammany Hall was able to influence the vote in particular among naturalized immigrants through its ward offices by offering a variety of services to the wards' constituents, for example help with official paperwork, job referrals, etc. The two issues of particular import in the present context are the organized crime link to politics and the criminogenic nature of immigrant societies, the latter because of their frail status in the host society.

This chapter has discussed the conceptual perceptions of organized crime and some of its particular characteristics. In the final part a case study considered the agitations of organized crime in one area and at a particular moment, and the next chapter will examine individual transnational crimes in more detail.

3 The transnational crimes

To a large degree, transnational crime consists in illicit trafficking in both illicit and licit product. The latter, illicit trafficking in licit product, is becoming a main source of income for transnational organized crime and its implications are not as well appreciated by most scholars as is the illicit traffic in illicit product; it will therefore be dealt with in some depth. The term *traffic* covers, as Mark Duffield notes, both illicit trade in illegal product and illicit trade in legal product; in fact, he operates with two related, but separate terms, *transborder trade* and *parallel trade*.[1] Transborder trade is a wider term than parallel trade, in so far as it encompasses both legal and illegal products, while parallel trade is the "informal" trade in products that are themselves legal. The most prominent product in illicit transnational trade in licit products is tobacco.[2]

The important increases in taxation of tobacco product have—in accordance with the concept denoted by *criminogenesis*—led to cigarette smuggling and unsuccessful supply-side enforcement efforts, for, as a number of economists, including Robin Thomas Naylor, have concluded, "never in history has there been a black market defeated from the supply side."[3] The subsection "Cigarette smuggling and organized crime" will examine the consequences of the fact that cigarette smuggling has now grown to a multi-billion dollar a year illegal enterprise linked to transnational organized crime and international terrorism. The chapter continues by an evaluation of the involvement of transnational organized crime in various other crime areas, such as credit card fraud, then examines the important issue of peacekeeping and organized crime, and finishes by observing, at some length, the fascinating case of one highly organized transnational crime group establishing itself on the territory of another, namely the establishment of Chinese organized crime in Italy.

The purpose of the chapter is three-fold; first, to familiarize the reader with some of the actual crimes that constitute the income flow for organized crime; second, to demonstrate the magnitude of the accrual of funds originating from what initially might seem minor transnational crime, such as the international smuggling of untaxed tobacco product; and, finally, to illustrate the pragmatism of horizontal, complementary cooperation between highly organized criminal groups. The thread, however, which runs through the chapter, is that of income generation for organized crime.

Illicit traffic in illicit product

This type of traffic is, as outlined in Chapter 2, relatively recent and it is fully dependent on the introduction of international prohibition regimes.[4] In today's world and in the context of transnational organized crime the most important illicit merchandise being trafficked is narcotic drugs, which will be treated, below. This particular international prohibition regime has—via the concept of criminogenesis discussed throughout this book—created a set of national, regional, and international problems, the scale of which is unparalleled in history: Exceedingly important profits for organized crime; high levels of micro-criminality as users are pushed toward prostitution and acquisitive crime; financing of terrorism and other organized criminal endeavors, etc. Without our underestimating the illicit traffic in other types of illicit product such as arms, the trafficking in narcotic drugs has nevertheless been chosen as illustrative.

Narcotic drugs

The trafficking of illicit drugs has been one of the main resource-generating activities of transnational organized crime since at least the 1970s. The line dividing production countries from consumption countries has become more and more blurred, one of the effects of which has been that the somewhat strident and incriminatory monologue by consumer countries directed at producer countries of the 1970s and 1980s has now assumed a more *pianissimo* tone and—with the realization that the problem is shared by all—has given room for a more appropriate dialogue.[5]

The treatment of the subject will, by necessity, be somewhat shorter than it warrants, first, because the literature on narcotics is immense and particularly interested readers can easily find very thorough treatments of each aspect of the subject-matter; and second, because an in-depth treatment of the narcotics subject would have placed undue emphasis on drug trafficking as opposed to many other illegal activities undertaken by transnational organized crime. I will argue that perhaps too much effort has been expended on this one, albeit very important area, rather than on other areas of illegal activities, which some scholars, the present one included, would consider equally or, indeed, more important. This is not necessarily because of the funds involved, but because of the diminution of human dignity (organized crime's management of the trafficking in humans and the, at least partially, related commercial sexual exploitation of children) or because the particular crime area represents "a clear and present danger" to humanity (organized crime involvement in deforestation and in trafficking in toxic waste and radioactive substances). Imbalance of attention generates a deficiency in analysis, which dislocates and so distorts the causal roles of differing types of evidence, leading to the generation of misleading conceptual identities.[6]

The illicit traffic in narcotic drugs is a so-called "prohibition regime," which furthermore is surprisingly recent. In other words, the international drug prohibition regime created a crime which hitherto had not existed. Never in the history of international law has so much effort been spent, so many conventions, treaties, bilateral and multinational memoranda of understanding signed and ratified, so many national, bilateral, regional, and international working groups and working relationships created, and so many public funds disbursed with so little result: the so-called War on Drugs, declared in 1971 by U.S. President Richard Nixon, has been lost and thoroughly lost. The proof of this conclusion resides in the truth that narcotic drugs today are available anywhere in the world, in particular in the Western world, of whatever variety, in whatever quantity, and of whatever purity. The table in Annex 2 indicates the retail prices of heroin from 1990 to 2006 in Europe and the United States. At the presentation of the 2006 International Narcotics Control Strategy Report,[7] the 23rd such yearly report, Anne W. Patterson, U.S. Assistant Secretary of State for International Narcotics and Law Enforcement Affairs, recognized that "narcotics are readily available," but added that "if we weren't doing these projects, the problem would be dramatically worse." One must respectfully ask how Patterson could possibly know what would have happened if something else had not happened. This is the kind of baseless speculation which unfortunately lies at the bottom of much ill-advised crime strategy. Moreover, the costs—in monetary terms—have been extremely high, as noted below.[8]

History

International drug control cooperation began in 1909 when the International Opium Commission, convened by the United States and attended by 13 world powers, met in Shanghai, China, leading to the signature in 1912 of the first international narcotics control convention, the Hague Opium Convention. The convention limited the manufacture, trade and use of these products to medical use; encouraged cooperation in order to restrict use and to enforce restriction efficiently; demanded the closure of opium dens; penalized possession; and prohibited selling to unauthorized persons.[9] A second International Opium Convention, concluded in 1925, established a Permanent Control Board, while the 1931 Geneva Convention for Limiting the Manufacture and Regulating the Distribution of Narcotic Drugs, introduced a compulsory estimates system and a Drug Supervisory Body to monitor the system.

After the end of the Second World War, the United Nations assumed the drug control function formerly carried out by the League of Nations—thus the Commission on Narcotic Drugs (CND) was created in 1946 as a functional commission of the Economic and Social Council (ECOSOC) and as the central policy-making body with regard to drugs. The Commission consisting of 53 members is a subsidiary body of the Economic and Social Council; it is the UN system's main policy-making organ for international drug control.[10]

The main control body, the International Narcotics Control Board (INCB) was created by the 1961 Convention on Narcotic Drugs. It is a 13-member board, which acts as the independent and quasi-judicial control organ for the implementation of UN drug conventions. The 13 individual members are elected in their personal capacity by the Economic and Social Council.

In 1991, the General Assembly of ECOSOC established the Fund of the United Nations International Drug Control Programme (UNDCP), through which the majority of the United Nations funds for narcotic drugs are managed, and it expanded the mandate of the Commission to enable it to function as the governing body of the program.

Three treaties now govern the international drug control system and require that governments exercise control over production and distribution, drug abuse, etc.: the Single Convention on Narcotic Drugs, 1961,[11] amended by the 1972 Protocol; the 1971 Convention on Psychotropic Substances;[12] and the 1988 United Nations Convention against Illicit Traffic in Narcotic Drugs and Psychotropic Substances.[13]

Costs of counter-measures

The costs of the so-called War on Drugs have been considerable since the declaration of the War in 1971. For the United States the expenditures at federal level are indicated in the table in Annex 3, which also outlines the split between funds disbursed on demand and supply reduction. U.S. anti-narcotics efforts consist of three pillars: (i) stopping use before it starts; (ii) healing America's drug users; and (iii) disrupting the market for illicit drugs.[14] For a critical view on U.S. drug expenditures, which claims that U.S. budget reporting is underreporting the total dispensed, as well as for an amusing watch, which shows second-by-second and year-to-date the funds dispensed by the government of the United States on the "war"—in accordance with the revised methodology of this organization—see the Drug Sense web site.[15] For 2009, the U.S. president has asked for $14.1 billion in federal funds in support of the three pillars of anti-narcotics efforts outlined above. If the split between federal and state expenditure retains the same proportionality as in 2008, which was 39.4 : 60.6, then the total (federal plus state) expenditures for 2009 on anti-narcotics programs will be $35.8 billion.

If by success one means a decrease in availability, these programs have not been successful. Indeed, from the declaration of the alleged War on Drugs in the early 1970s, supply of opium has steadily risen from approximately 1,000 tons per year to almost 8,000 tons.[16] Rensselaer Lee notes candidly that "(S)upply reduction has been an unmitigated failure, at least as judged by trends in the US marketplace. Per gram prices of cocaine and heroin dropped by approximately two-thirds between 1981 and 1996, while purity of these drugs increased respectively by 44 percent and 83 percent."[17]

There are several explanations for this total failure, the most intriguing of which was provided by the scholar Alfred McCoy,[18] who pointed out that the major miscalculation of the heavily law-enforcement-based alleged War on Drugs strategy and an essential explanatory component of its failure is that decision makers wrongly assumed that supply of narcotic drugs is non-flexible, meaning that repression of trade in illegal narcotics would be an effective measure to decrease it, whereas in reality it is demand which is inelastic. Therefore, the supply side efforts by the United Nations and the United States have been "in defiance of the basic dynamics of global drug supply" and were bound to fail from the very beginning. Other scholars, for example Christina Jacqueline Johns, are persuaded that the War on Drugs and its continuance even in the face of continual defeat is explainable by the fact that "The War on Drugs is a tool in a larger war that is about increased authority and social control."[19] Although she is right in observing a strategy of increased societal control and militarized internal security, yet a more prosaic explanation was provided by Max Weber discussing institutional survival and auto-multiplication.

Institutions, be they a law enforcement agency or the department of criminology in a university, first and foremost concentrate on their own survival, and not, respectively, on policing or research into criminal justice. The larger such bureaucratic machines (law enforcement, university, etc.) become, the more unstoppable their institutional inertia and the more pronounced their capacity for self-creation.[20]

It is a remarkable fact that the international narcotics policy agenda has been driven by the United States since its very inception in 1909 with the countries of the rest of the world following more or less willingly. As noted throughout this subsection, the so-called War on Drugs has been a failure in general, but even more so has it when waged on the international scene. Lee judges this international drug enforcement effort harshly: "America's so-called war against drugs in the 1980s and the 1990s has been a conspicuous foreign policy fiasco."[21] The curious and unhelpful intermingling of U.S. national law enforcement and foreign policy commenced as a result of the recommendations of the 1983 President's Commission on Law Enforcement and the Administration of Justice, which in the words of Adam Edwards and Peter Gill "hypothecated US 'foreign assistance' policy to the control of organized crime."[22] This approach to foreign policy has complicated relations with a number of countries, in particular in the Caribbean and in Central and South America, since the central issue in such relations became drug enforcement.[23] Such a fixation on supply side interdiction against demand side reduction in the face of scientific analysis can be seen as having an obvious racial or xenophobe undertone, reducing the problem to an external threat by foreigners and thus avoiding having to recognize that the drug problem is in the Bronx as well as among Manhattan's yuppy population, and not in Bolivia or Burma. The scientific data were quite robust already in 1994, when a Rand Corporation narcotics study found that $34 million invested in treatment reduced cocaine use as much as $783 million spent on overseas counter-narcotics programs and $366 million spent on interdiction.[24]

To examine the international traffic in narcotic drugs in any details would exceed the dimensions of the present work; therefore, quantitative information has been placed in the Annexes in table form. Here only a few general trends will be treated. Seizures of cocaine reached an all-time high in 2004 with 588 tons, most of which (86 percent) was seized in the Americas and almost all the rest in Europe (13 percent). The main route now leads from the Andean countries (Bolivia, Peru, and Colombia) to North America. The coca pasta is obtained from Bolivia and Peru and transformed to cocaine in Colombia. The new development is that the main target area for Colombia no longer is

North America, but Mexico. Organized crime in Mexico transports the drugs across country from the south to the north, and then into the United States. Mexican organized crime has also been supplanting Colombian criminal groups in the south and mid-western United States to control wholesale cocaine distribution. The Caribbean therefore is becoming increasingly less important for international cocaine trafficking into the United States, whereas the region retains its importance for the cocaine traffic towards Europe.

Illicit traffic in licit product

It is not immediately clear that Duffield's classification (see beginning of Chapter 3) of transborder trade is very helpful, since all three sub-species (illicit trade in illicit product, illicit trade in legal product, and illicit trade in illegally obtained legal product) are fully within the managerial sphere of organized crime. Since, however, the illicit trade in legal product is less well known than illicit traffic in illegal product, and since income generated from this activity nourishes the international flows of monetary funds of non-declared origin—and thus both transnational organized crime and terrorism—the most prominent and most lucrative product in illicit transnational trade, tobacco, is considered in the following.

Cigarette smuggling

In Europe and elsewhere, for example in the United States, governments have substantially increased the amount of taxes paid on tobacco products, partly—allegedly—to discourage their use, partly to raise revenue.[25] It is evident that the customs and similar revenue-raising regulations have a strong criminogenic effect, which has the same unintended consequences as UN Security Council sanctions, namely to create a parallel market. This is gratefully satisfied by criminal organizations, who deliver smuggled tobacco products at a lower price than that imposed by governments and, lately, counterfeit tobacco product. Cigarettes are the world's most widely smuggled legal consumer product: Each year 400 billion cigarettes or one-third of all legally exported cigarettes in the world are smuggled.[26]

Cigarettes, and in particular brand cigarettes, can be considered not only a commodity, but also a currency; the product has been de-reified and its price basically represents a monetary value equal to the imposed tax.[27] It is therefore not surprising that cigarettes have been and are being smuggled to exploit the arbitrage mentioned above, nor that cigarettes—like other currencies—are being counterfeited. Indeed, the anecdotal evidence of Italian organized crime smuggling untaxed cigarettes across the Adriatic Sea from Yugoslavia in fast motor vessels are legion and most travelers to Italy have been offered "duty-free" cigarettes by ambulant sellers in trains and on the street, particularly in ports such as Naples and Genoa.

More surprising, however, is the alleged involvement of the tobacco industry in the smuggling activities. Suspicions of tobacco industry involvement in cigarette smuggling have grown since 1997 when researchers demonstrated, by comparing annual global exports with global imports, that about a third of all cigarettes entering international markets each year could not be accounted for.[28] From approximately 1992, tobacco companies experienced difficulties in increasing sales of their brand cigarettes in the high-income markets in the Western world and determined that the reason, or a contributing reason, was the high retail price caused by the very heavy duties levied by the governments of the countries concerned. Smuggling is an operationally effective reaction and one that does not entail any moral opprobrium, since many— in particular poorer smokers—understandably perceive the high duties as unjustly targeting them and they therefore see smugglers of tobacco products not as criminals but rather as individuals doing "the people" a favor.[29]

The British government claims that about one in every three cigarettes smoked is smuggled; indeed, in 2000, British customs officers seized a record 2 billion smuggled cigarettes compared with 1.3 billion in 1999. After Britain imposed steep tax increases on cigarettes sold in the United Kingdom in the beginning of the 1990s, exports to Andorra from the United Kingdom suddenly increased from 13 million cigarettes in 1993 to 1.52 billion in 1997. This represented a 116-fold increase and a 140-a-day habit for every man, woman and child in Andorra. Spanish and Andorran Customs stopped the tax-free imports and by January 1998, British exports to Andorra had dried up. They were, however, only redirected to Cyprus where 435 million British cigarettes were shipped annually before Andorra was closed to smugglers, according to U.K. press reports, but in 2001 this number increased to about 6 billion British brand cigarettes, even though the island has only 700,000 people. British customs believes that the vast majority of exports to these two destinations ended up right back in Great Britain, brought in by a number of criminal organizations.[30]

Cigarette smuggling and organized crime

There is little doubt that organized crime is involved in the illicit trade in tobacco products, and it has been for as long as governments have used these products as a convenient way of raising revenue. In 2000, then U.S. Customs Commissioner Raymond W. Kelly stated that "Profits from cigarette smuggling rival those of narcotic trafficking" and that "the United States plays an important role as a source and transshipment country." He also claimed, that "International cigarette smuggling has grown to a multi-billion dollar a year illegal enterprise linked to transnational organized crime and international terrorism."

However, some organized crime would appear to have moved from the smuggling of narcotic drugs, arms, and people to smuggling cigarettes; while the profits are roughly the same,[31] yet the risk of being apprehended is much lower, and the sentences, if apprehended, considerably lighter. As one law enforcement officer working in the Balkans said: "What people in our business sometimes forget is that if serious criminals move from smuggling drugs, people or guns into cigarettes, that might be a better thing from everyone's point of view."[32]

The involvement of organized crime in the illicit cigarette trade and its sometimes international character was demonstrated in August 2002, when the U.S. authorities partially by chance disrupted a sophisticated smuggling operation: customs inspectors in Miami discovered more than $300,000 worth of false tobacco tax stamps manufactured in Paraguay en route for New York.[33]

Tobacco manufacturers often claim that the international smuggling of their products is the work of international organized crime. That is undoubtedly true; however, an in-depth inquiry by the Center for Public Integrity[34] seems to indicate that tobacco company officials at British American Tobacco (BAT), Philip Morris, and R. J. Reynolds have worked closely with companies and individuals directly connected to organized crime in Hong Kong, Canada, Colombia, Italy, and the United States. From an academic—and indeed prosecutorial—point of view, the almost insurmountable difficulty becomes to prove the level of knowledge on the part of top management. The most disturbing fact, however, is that on many occasions former tobacco industry executives have set themselves up as wholesale dealers, but, in fact, act as a cut-out function between the tobacco industry and organized crime. This seems to happen so often that one can legitimately ask oneself if it is a coincidence or a carefully planned governance pattern.

The Tommy Chui case

Tommy Chui was a former director of BAT's biggest distributor of contraband cigarettes to China and Taiwan. In 1995, he was scheduled to be the leading prosecutorial witness in a prosecution in Hong Kong brought by Hong Kong's Independent Commission Against Corruption (ICAC) concerning a $1.2 billion smuggling operation to China and Taiwan. The case itself implicated three former BAT executives in a HK$100 million ($12.8 million) bribery scandal, as well as the bribing of Chui's two former business associates, corrupt customs officers, and alleged members of the triads. On 29 March 1995, his body was found in the harbor of Singapore.[35] He had been abducted, ritually tortured, suffocated, and thrown into the harbor "just weeks before he was to testify against his ex-associates."[36]

The counterfeiting of brand cigarettes

In July 2005, authorities in Ghana seized 100 million counterfeit cigarettes carrying the Philip Morris International trademark "Marlboro." They were seized in shipping containers in transit for Europe, having been shipped from China under the trade declaration "sports shoes." A year later, 2006–7, Bulgarian security sources claimed that they seized container loads of counterfeit cigarettes arriving from Dubai, but allegedly manufactured in China.[37] In fact, the World Customs Organization estimates the annual production of counterfeit cigarettes in the PRC at 190 billion. Furthermore, sources at the World Customs Organization (WCO) have informed the present author that there is a clear increase in the seizures of counterfeit cigarettes within the European Community. This is hardly surprising, since the demand for low-price tobacco product persists and will be met by an adequate supply. If this, at least temporarily, cannot be sourced from the tobacco industry itself, it will be met with counterfeit product (see Table 3.1).

According to the European Anti-Fraud Office (OLAF), 65 percent of all cigarettes smuggled in the world are now counterfeit and of these, according to the WCO, more than half are produced in China.[38]

Cigarette smuggling and terrorism

Considering the arbitrage made possible by the price differential on a popular, legal consumer good between countries and, indeed, even within a country such as the United States ($7.50 in New York City; $4.62 in Long Island), it is hardly surprising that also terrorists have used—and presumably are using—cigarette smuggling to raise funds. A number of cases have come to attention so far.

On 21 January 2002, in Charlotte, North Carolina, 25 individuals were indicted for moving cigarettes by rental vehicles from Charlotte to Detroit, Michigan, where they sold the tobacco products in the

Table 3.1 Origin of counterfeit cigarettes, 2006

Country	Percent
China	59.9
UAE[1]	10.8
Poland	5.5
Malaysia	3.5
Ukraine	3.3
Russia	3.2
Romania	3.0
Indonesia	2.5
Greece	2.4
Other	6.1

Source: WCO.
Note: It is possible that most of the counterfeit cigarettes seized in or coming
  from the UAE originate in China and only transited the UAE.

streets, exploiting the price differential between the two states. Proceeds
were then transferred by wire and by courier to Beirut, Lebanon.[39] At
the time of the offences, there was a price differential between North
Carolina, where the cigarette tax was \$0.50 per carton, and Michigan,
where the same tax was \$7.50 per carton. The two individuals exploi-
ted this differential by trafficking cigarettes of a total value of \$7.5
million from North Carolina to Michigan with a resultant revenue loss
of \$3 million for the state of Michigan. Some of the proceeds were
donated to Hezbollah, an organization which the U.S. State Department
has placed on a list of foreign terrorist organizations.[40]

Also, counterfeit cigarette tax stamps were found in an apartment in
New York, United States, used by members of the Egyptian Islamic Jihad
cell that carried out the 1993 bombing of the World Trade Center.[41]
Furthermore, one of the individuals, who was accused of being part of an
al-Qaeda sleeper cell outside Buffalo, N.Y., had a criminal history involving the smuggling of cigarettes, also known as cigarette bootlegging.[42]

These three cases should be read in conjunction with the case study
"Operation Green Quest" in order for one of the main tenets and
implications of this book to be fully appreciated: international terrorism, like organized crime, is financed, not by large, sophisticated,
international and electronic transfers of funds, but by a continuous
trickle of funds originating from the kind of common crime that does
not attract much attention from law enforcement, because of the sheer
number of individual acts; examples are organized retail theft and
cigarette smuggling. For illustrative purposes, one could consider each
minimalist operation (group) as a tap, from which spouts not water,

but money (not liquid, but liquidity). There are many such taps, all nourished by the proceeds from common crime; it is, however, not possible to distinguish the taps whose flows are destined for terrorism, from those destined to enrich common or organized criminals, or to fund further criminal activity. This form of funding represents several distinctive characteristics: (i) *Invisibility*: the individual criminal acts are invisible, exactly because there are too many of them[43] and the quantities and values involved in each individual instance do not attract law enforcement attention; (ii) *Immunity*: even if one or more individual funding taps are closed by law enforcement activity, in the overall funding structure, such disruption would be negligible; (iii) *Self-repair*: since the demand subsists, any non-identified member of the closed-down tap can step in and re-open the tap.

Other transnational organized crime

Transnational organized crime is involved in a number of crimes at national and international level. Common to them is—as the wife of a Brooklyn Mafioso stated about her husband—the basic goal of all their activities, namely "manipulating people out of their money."[44] Apart from the narcotic drugs and cigarette smuggling, considered above, transnational organized crime has found a number of other criminal activities to do just that. Some of these will be considered below, namely cyber-delinquency, credit card fraud, and trafficking in humans. One should keep in mind, though, that the human imagination is unlimited, in particular when it comes to "manipulating people out of their money."

Cyber-delinquency

The use of modern storage and communication technology, and in particular the Internet, is an important aspect of modern crime. Such delinquency is very often transnational, because of the very structure of the World Wide Web; one is reminded of Bossard's opinion quoted in Chapter 1 about the "intention", which renders the crime international. However fanciful "cyber" sounds one should recall that one is discussing a means; "pen and paper" sounds less exciting ("paper-delinquency"), but more crime, including transnational organized crime, is presumably done by the use of the latter rather than the former.

There are several references to cyber-delinquency throughout this volume; at this point, therefore, only the issue of so-called "e-fencing" will be considered. In the United States, annual losses to organized retail crime are approximately $30 billion. Therefore, a section below deals, inter alia, with organized "fencing," a crime which now has become very common within the ambit of cyber-delinquency, namely where online "auction sites" are being used by professional retail criminals to off-load stolen goods. The U.S. Congress has studied means to constrain online auction sites to control access to their sites, in particular by high-volume sellers[45] and on 15 July 2008, a proposed Organized Retail Crime Act of 2008 was introduced and referred to the House Committee on the Judiciary.[46] This proposed Act would make organized retail crime a federal offense and would place responsibility on online sites, such as eBay, to investigate suspicious transactions and to request and store for three years the names and addresses of high-volume sellers.

Credit card fraud

Over the last half century payments in cash have slowly been replaced with non-cash payments, such as checks, direct debit and, in particular, the use of credit cards. Such usage has, obviously, given rise to extensive misuse. For this particular crime, the situation in the United Kingdom will first be examined, followed by two short case studies, namely: (i) a U.S. case believed to be the largest automated teller machine (ATM) fraud in history and linked to transnational organized crime; and (ii) an international case underlining some very remarkable characteristics, including international cooperation between organized crime groups, and speed of execution.

In the United Kingdom, at the end of 2007, 145 million cards (72 million debit cards; 73 million credit and charge cards) had been issued; there were 9.9 billion transactions in 2007 for a total value of £567.7 billion. Also in 2007, there were 2.8 billion withdrawals of cash through 63,420 ATMs for a total of £186 billion or £5,898 per second.[47] A table indicating the various forms of credit card fraud committed in the period between 1997 and 2007 can be found in Annex 7. In the context of transnational organized crime, the overall structure of credit card fraud in the 10-year period in question leads to a number of observations.

As one would suspect, the number of so-called card not present (CNP) frauds, that is to say frauds committed, where the credit or debit card was not present, and as the result of the theft of genuine bank details, and which are transacted via telephone, Internet, or mail order has increased to £290.5 million for 2007 and now constitutes the largest type of bank fraud in the United Kingdom. One should, however, recall that although in the period from 2000 to 2007 this crime increased by 298 percent, the value of such transactions in the same period increased by 871 percent, from £3.5 billion in 2000 to 34 billion in 2007. In the context of CNP frauds it is worth noting that a number of chat rooms exist where stolen card details are bought and sold. When a card number is posted, it is typically "maxed out" and purchases have been made totaling the allowed maximum for the card, within nine minutes.[48] Credit card numbers are obtained by, often transnational, "phishing" web sites that are copies of online banking web sites or advantageous online offers inducing the user to enter his or her credit card details in order to purchase the—non-existent—merchandise. Table 3.2 indicates the number of phishing web sites targeting U.K. banks over the last three years, month by month. The increase is amazing; thus in December 2007, 3,195 such phishing sites were identified against 1,513 in December 2006 and 353 in December 2005.

ATM fraud occurs when funds are fraudulently withdrawn from ATMs. In the United Kingdom, the amounts lost are relatively modest compared with other types of card fraud; however, ATM machines are also used to obtain card details, typically in one of three ways: (i) *card-trapping devices* (card trapped in device introduced in card slot, criminal tricks customers to re-enter their personal identification number (PIN); eventually, customer gives up and leaves; criminal retrieves card and now has card plus PIN); (ii) *skimming devices* register electronic details from magnetic strip, while the PIN is obtained by the use of a concealed miniature camera; and (iii) *shoulder surfing*: as shown in the case study, below, "A massive ATM fraud," this type of crime has attracted the attention of internationally operating organized crime .

From the point of view of transnational organized crime, the most interesting type of credit card fraud is the counterfeiting of credit cards. This card fraud type reached a peak in 2001—the year chip-and-PIN security was introduced in the United Kingdom—and then diminished as was expected. In 2007, however, the losses reached £144 million, almost the same as at the peak. Perusal of Table 3.3 provides

Table 3.2 Numbers of phishing websites targeted against U.K. banks, 2004–07

		Month											
		Jan	Feb	Mar	Apr	May	Jun	Jul	Aug	Sep	Oct	Nov	Dec
	2007	1290	974	1130	1188	1274	1368	3066	3268	2597	3170	3277	3195
Year	2006	606	669	1074	947	919	872	970	1484	1513	1596	1993	1513
	2005	18	29	27	54	72	122	153	160	190	267	255	353

Source: APACS, *Fraud: The Facts 2008* (London: APACS, 2008), 45.

Table 3.3 Counterfeit card fraud, U.K.-issued cards, U.K. and abroad, 2004–07

£ millions	2004	2005	2006	2007
U.K.	105.9	78.6	45.8	31.1
Abroad	23.8	18.2	52.8	113.2

Source: APACS, *Fraud: The Facts 2008* (London: APACS, 2008), 11.

an explanation: As the losses to counterfeit fraud diminishes over the four years, 2004–7, for U.K. cards used in the United Kingdom (from £105.9 million in 2004 to £31.1 million in 2007), it increases considerably for U.K.-issued cards used abroad (from £23.8 million in 2004 to £113.2 million in 2007).

Case study: a massive ATM fraud

An individual, reportedly linked to Albanian-Yugoslav organized crime, after being deported from the United States for a series of serious crimes, soon returned and in 2000 initiated the presumably largest ATM fraud ever committed in the United States and possibly in the world.[49]

He took advantage of the fact that little or no background checks were performed on individuals or companies wishing to enter the private ATM market. He bought a number of ATMs of the kind normally found in delicatessen shops, restaurants, etc., which he equipped with skimming devices, whereupon he installed them. He skimmed personal bank account information from at least 21,000 people, which he, in 2001 and 2002, used to make ATM cards allowing him to withdraw $3.5 million from regular bank ATMs. Since 2001, the U.S. Secret Service has seized a total of approximately 60 ATM machines from New York, Florida, and Michigan allegedly used by this person and his associates.

Case study: a credit card fraud

As underlined in Chapter 2 concerning the management talent of organized crime in general and transnational crime in particular, this case study is a very clear demonstration of two concepts of crucial importance in the understanding of the subject-matter, *organizational talent* and *speed of execution*, both part of organized crime viewed as business and as such linked to the economics of crime.[50] To illustrate the two points, the reader is referred to Table 3.4, which depicts a

Table 3.4 A credit card scheme

Step	Where	What	Who	Time of Execution
1	West Coast, USA	Credit card swiped under the counter; credit card information obtained. Electronic transfer to: ↓	Vietnamese gang members working 'on contract' for HK triad	0
2	Hong Kong	Collation Ship by air:	Triad	3
3	Kuala Lumpur	Production of false credit cards with information from US cards. Ship by air: ↓		
4	Milan, Italy	Reception of cards.[1] Transhipment by air: ↓	Camorra, Neapolitan organised crime (who "has the client")	27
5	Prague, Czechoslovakia	Reception. Dispatch of agents who are to use cards for purchases ↓	Russian Organized Crime	61
6	London, Paris, Rome	Purchase of luxury goods by agents almost to $20,000 limit of cards. By air: ↓	Agents acting for Russian Organized Crime in Prague	123
7	Prague, Czechoslovakia	Delivery of goods. Then by truck: ↓	Agents of Russian OC organizers	181
8	Moscow, Russia	Sale to shops	Gum Store, Red Square	200

(Time of Execution: Hours from initial act, i.e. credit card swipe)
Source: Jeffrey Robinson, *The Merger: The Conglomeration of International Organized Crime* (Woodstock, NY: The Overlock Press, 2000), 21–23.
Note: Cards concealed inside cigarette packs, which were resealed, placed in resealed duty-free cigarette cartons, and carried, along with a duty-free bottle of alcohol, in "duty-free plastic bags" as transported by a large number of international travellers.

factual credit card fraud. Column 2 read from top to bottom provides a series of events, while column 4 is the time line in hours counted from the initial criminal act on the West Coast of the United States.

At hour 0, a Vietnamese shopkeeper in California, working with organized crime performs a "double sweep" by sweeping the customer's credit card through the credit card machine on top of the desk and, while detracting the customer's attention, a second time in a credit card reader under the desk. This second reader only stores the credit card information; it does not transmit it. Once the customer has left the shop, the information is electronically transferred to organized crime in Hong Kong, where it is collated with information from other credit cards obtained simultaneously from other operatives in the United States. The information is then trans-shipped to Kuala Lumpur, Malaysia, where it is embossed on false credit cards. These are sent via courier by air to Milan, Italy, where the Neapolitan organized crime group, the Camorra, takes control of them. They are then sold and brought by air to Russian organized crime in Prague, Czechoslovakia. From here a number of "purchasers" are sent to the luxury goods shops in Paris, Rome, and London, where each shopper buys articles totaling almost, but not quite, the credit card maxima. The goods are then flown to Moscow, Russia, for sale in a shop on the Red Square, where they are available at hour 200.

There are a number of major observations to be made from this case: First, pragmatic cooperation between organized crime groups, namely Hong Kong organized crime (Triads), Italian organized crime (the Camorra), and Russian organized crime. It should be emphasized that such cooperation is horizontal, among equals; it is not the result of a fiat from a supranational crime director or directorate. In fact, *networking* is arguably a sounder term than organization.

Second, the international production line, with parts of the operation being executed in various countries, mimics the organization of production in a modern multinational company. It obviously thwarts any attempt at interruption of the activity in real time, as well as at investigation of same ex-post, and it poses innumerable legal problems should prosecution be attempted.

Third, the *speed of execution* is such that very few, if any, legitimate commercial companies could match it. The speed obviously reduces any possibility of discovery in the course of execution of the criminal conspiracy, since the handling of the incriminating material on each step is the shortest possible.

Fourth, one observes a certain level of *specialization*. Step 3 in Table 3.4 indicates that the false credit cards were manufactured in Kuala

Lumpur. Already in 1991, the French authorities identified trafficking in false credit cards from Kuala Lumpur. The criminal activities were then directed by a triad from Hong Kong (see step 2 in Table 3.4), but they used Francophone overseas Chinese from Vietnam and Cambodia to use the cards for purchases throughout France.[51]

Finally, questions have been raised, but never adequately answered, as to the *organizational talents and capabilities* inherent in an operation of this type. Indeed, such skills are rare outside of the top-level multinational corporate world. In this context, one can also adduce the organizational skills involved in distributing counterfeit consumer goods, for example luxury watches, from production in the Far East to informal retail trade basically all over the Western world,[52] involving seamless cooperation between individuals of many different cultural backgrounds, stretching from the, typically, Chinese manufacturer in the PRC to the, typically, sub-Saharan salesperson on the streets of, say, Western Europe.

One of the management techniques this kind of organized crime organization seems to have adopted successfully is "Just in Time" (JIT). In the corporate world, this refers to a strict management of warehouse inventories; to cut down on inventories and therefore on the financial cost of warehousing caused by an increase in stock, sub-contractors and suppliers are requested to supply materials and semi-finished goods at the shortest notice possible before the goods are used in production. Organized crime seems to use the same techniques, partly, it can be presumed, for the same reasons, namely cost-cutting, but partly, and presumably more importantly, to cut down on the time the organization is in possession of incriminating materials, in the course of which the organization is in its most vulnerable position.

In summary form: highly efficient, intercultural, networked cooperative capabilities comparable to the most efficient modern management techniques. Without needing to be overly philosophical, one might surmise that organized crime in its entrepreneurial aspects in some way is mimetic in respect of transnational enterprises and their techniques, from global supply lines to jurisdictional arbitrage.

Trafficking in humans

The two terms, *Smuggling of Humans* and *Trafficking in Persons*, indicate two different crimes that are the object of two different protocols to CATOC. Nevertheless, they often overlap: in theory people smuggling consists of the illegal transport across borders of migrants against remuneration. The latter is sometimes paid prior to the criminal act and there is no further need for contact between the smuggled person and the smuggling entity. In practice, however, migrants cannot pay the smuggling fee and therefore establish an indenture agreement whereby they pay the debt—in installments—once they have arrived in the target country, thereby in reality becoming part of trafficking in persons, rather than people smuggling. The current (2008) fees would appear to be €4,000 to be smuggled from Kosovo to Vienna, Austria, and $16,000 from Bosnia to any destination in the European Union.[53]

The designation *trafficking in persons* also, more informally, termed *trafficking in humans*, encompasses the activities of forced labor and of commercial sexual exploitation. The latter perhaps is better known from the media, but one should not underestimate the harsh conditions under which the former have to toil, often for many years and without pay; common for both is that the majority of such persons are trafficked internationally and mostly by relatively well-established, albeit often small criminal organizations. In the context of the present work, trafficking in humans is important since it generates substantial revenues. Indeed, as Francis Miko demonstrates, such trafficking is currently presumably the third largest source of income for criminal organizations of various kinds, besides the illicit traffic in narcotics and illicit arms sales; and it is most certainly the fastest growing:[54]

Trafficking in humans is increasingly perpetrated by organized, sophisticated criminal enterprises. Such trafficking is the fastest growing source of profits for organized criminal enterprises worldwide. Profits from the trafficking industry contribute to the expansion of organized crime in the United States and worldwide.[55]

Trafficking in persons shares certain dynamics with alien smuggling in that both involve the moving of human beings, but it is different in having the additional element of coercion or exploitation.[56]

On the international level, *trafficking in persons* is defined in Article 3(a) of the United Nations Protocol to Prevent, Suppress and Punish Trafficking in Persons, Especially Women and Children, Supplementing the United Nations Convention Against Transnational Organized Crime.[57] The UN definition is quoted in its entirety:

"Trafficking in persons" shall mean the recruitment, transportation, transfer, harbouring or receipt of persons, by means of the threat or use of force or other forms of coercion, of abduction, of fraud, of deception, of the abuse of power or of a position of vulnerability or of the giving or receiving of payments or benefits to achieve the consent of a person having control over another person, for the purpose of exploitation. Exploitation shall include, at a minimum, the exploitation of the prostitution of others or other forms of sexual exploitation, forced labour or services, slavery or practices similar to slavery, servitude or the removal of organs.

Although precise numbers are difficult to obtain, without expressing any undue subjectivity, I would maintain that the number of individuals who are victims of this traffic is astonishing; thus, according to the United Nations Children's Fund (UNICEF),[58] some 2 million children in the world work as prostitutes. A Swedish NGO found in 2001 that 500,000 women are trafficked to the European Union (EU) sex market per year (EU then 15 countries)[59] which seems relatively high, although in the EU, the Netherlands has seen the sharpest increase in trafficking in humans for prostitution, reaching 30,000 per year already in 1997 and undoubtedly increasing (see Table 3.5).

The traffic in humans has now reached such a level that a number of scholars are comparing it to the traffic in African slaves; they term traffic in humans *modern slavery* or *neo-slavery*. These writers point out that modern slavery is more important, in absolute terms, than the Atlantic slave trade: "Whatever the exact number is, it seems almost certain that the modern global slave trade is larger in absolute terms than the Atlantic slave trade in the eighteenth and nineteenth centuries was."[60] This argument will not be carried any further, since I object to the quantification of misery: If an activity is recognized as inhuman (a crime against humanity), as are genocide and slavery,[61] the numerical comparison of singular aspects of such activities are, I would argue, not only irrelevant but also offensive.

Ethan Kapstein notes that according to the U.S. government, 600–800,000 persons are coerced into forced labor every year, of which 80 percent are female, 50 percent are under the age of 18, 43 percent are forced into the sex trade, and 32 percent into unpaid labor. The UN

Table 3.5 Entries, yearly, into Dutch prostitution markets

1980	2,500
1989	20,000
1997	30,000

Source: Richard Poulin, "Prostitution, crime organisé et marchandisation," *Revue Tiers Monde*, XLIV, no. 176 (2003): 737.

calculates the annual income to human traffickers at approximately $10 billion and the average price of each trafficked human to be $12,500, of which $3,000 represents costs. Kapstein emphasizes that the cost of a slave today is much less than that of an African slave brought to the United States, and he explains this decrease in price by the less onerous transportation available today.[62]

The criminal motivation for the sex industry is obviously first and foremost revenue; worldwide the sex industry generates profits of $7–12 billion over and above those accruing to the traffickers, estimated at $10 billion. A particularly alarming subset of this industry is constituted by the so-called commercial sexual exploitation of children. It may initially seem an area which is shocking but involving a limited number of persons. However, a recent study from the United States has disclosed a number of highly disquieting facts:[63]

- Of all sexual assaults, 66.9 percent were committed against juveniles (individuals under the age of 18). Of the 66.9 percent sexual assaults on juveniles, one half (34.1 percent of total) were on children under the age of 12.
- Whereas *forcible rape* is committed primarily against persons in the two age groups from 12 to 17 and from 18 to 24, *forcible sodomy* is almost exclusively committed against juveniles, 78.8 percent against persons under the age of 18 and 54.8 percent against persons under the age of 12.
- *Sexual assault with an object* is also a crime committed mainly against juveniles. Of such assaults, 75.2 percent are committed against persons under the age of 18, and 49.7 percent against persons under the age of 12.

Commercial sexual exploitation of children probably has more international ramifications than any other crime except the illicit traffic in drugs, as pointed out by Daniel Campagna and Donald Poffenberger.[64] On the international level, this crime has three major aspects, which although interconnected must be considered separately: The international sale of children from one country to another for sexual exploitation; the international travel of individuals who seek to engage in sexual activities with children in a foreign jurisdiction; and the international dissemination of child pornography, in particular via the Internet.

Children are being trafficked internationally for many reasons, including to serve as forced labor, in the illicit adoption trade, etc. There are, however, overlaps, since the child who is imported into a country to serve as domestic labor, often is raped by the person he or she works for and then passed on to the sex industry. Likewise, a certain number of adoptions, international transfers into shelters for street children and into orphanages are, in reality, camouflage for the misuse of these children by pedophiles, who, inter alia because of increased law enforcement activities on national level, are being forced to use more and more elaborate schemes to ensure the presence of the children on whom they are fixated. So-called sex tourism centered on children represents a particularly difficult problem set from an enforcement point of view.

In the early 1970s, pornography was at its zenith, in particular in the Scandinavian countries and in the Netherlands, and by the mid-1970s, commercially distributed child pornography became widely available in the United States and Europe. Modern technology has had a deep impact on the production, distribution, and possession of child pornography. First, by using relatively inexpensive equipment and software, it is now possible in a private setting to register visual depictions of children in a sexual context (to use the Interpol definition[65]) and to transmit the registration from the handheld registration medium, for example a Camcorder, to the hard disk of a computer. Once the images are fixed on the hard drive, it is then possible to distribute them discreetly via electronic mail and, what constitutes a worrying novelty, such digital images can be reproduced indefinitely without loss of picture quality. Also, modern electronic compression and storage facilities allow the possessor to store very large quantities on one recordable compact disc (CD) or one universal serial bus (USB) mass storage device, not to mention the amount of feed that can be stored on a removable hard disk drive. Furthermore, already existing (original) photographs can be scanned into the computer memory and distributed as indicated above. A fair amount of child pornography which is available on the Internet, in fact consists of photographs dating back 20–30 years.

The environment and transnational organized crime

Transnational organized crime is—worryingly—deeply involved in crimes against the environment, and this in several ways. This section will concentrate on the illicit exploitation of forest resources with subsequent deforestation as a result, while a subsequent section deals with the involvement of organized crime in the transnational disposal of waste, in particular toxic waste.

The natural resources of the earth are restricted commodities; they are therefore coveted and traded by organized crime. Diamonds, and in particular so-called "conflict diamonds" constitute an example, as does coltan (used for electronic devices), but still more insidious is the involvement of organized crime in the illicit trade in timber.

Hardwood in particular has become a restricted commodity as more and more producer countries are attempting to manage the remaining stock. The illicit traffic in timber lies, however, first and foremost in the ambit of organized crime, since the latter can apply the necessary pressure on the local population—in conjunction with extensive corruption to police or military personnel—and provide the managerial expertise to have the trees felled, transported internationally by ship, and sold in another country often with false documentation of origin. In Southeast Asia, where most of the world's remaining high-value hardwood grows, the "organizers" pay $11 to the local population per cubic meter of illegally logged hardwood and then resell the same logs in another country in the region for up to $270 (factory gate price). The logs are then cut into planks and used, in particular, for floorboards at a mark-up on the factory gate price of approximately 500 percent. The profits accruing to organized crime are staggering, even considering that the criminals pay an average of $200,000 in corruption payments for each shipload. Apart from the societal damage usually connected with organized crime—corruption, lack of respect for the rule of law, etc.—this particular commodity also entails revenue losses and environmental costs to the producer countries.

It is difficult to hold an uneducated, exceedingly poor lumberjack responsible for the acts whereby he earns a meager living for himself and his family, whereas the responsibility for the international traffic in illicitly logged timber fully lies with the end-users, who import or allow the importation of such merchandise, while fully cognizant of the fact that at least 50 percent of it is illegal at source. It is worth recalling from a previous discussion in this book that economists[66] are agreed that *no gray market has ever been defeated from the supply side*, which is what the Western World attempts to do in this regard as in many others. This is at best a case of willful blindness or, indeed, an example of the application of deviant knowledge in the sense that the importing governments know as well as the mentioned economists that such markets cannot be suppressed from the supply side. If they insist on a supply side approach, one must surmise that it is because other, domestic, forces are so strong that efforts on the demand side are—economically and therefore politically—unacceptable.

If one were to accept a definition of "organized crime" postulating as its main characteristic "the trade in prohibited or restricted merchandise," then illegal logging and the transportation and commercialization of wood and forestry product, which is illegal at source, is organized crime. A chain of operators intervenes in the international trade in illegal timber ("illegal at source") from lumberjack to consumer, as the logged timber is traded, transported, transformed (from round logs to planks), and commercialized. Because of the important bulk-to-value ratio, it is relatively easy for interested observers from concerned NGOs to follow the forest products from forest to end user.

The products here under consideration often are either totally or partially prohibited for exportation. In Indonesia, ramin[67] is on the Cites II schedule with export prohibition,[68] and as regards merbau,[69] only forest product, but not logs, may be exported. Furthermore, since logs more often than not are illegal at source and therefore acquired without permission from owner and without payment of appropriate dues, the only way to export such products and thus to enter into the lucrative international markets is by transborder trade. The concept of *transborder trade* should be distinguished from that of *parallel* or *informal trade*. The legality of the commodities involved in transborder trade is a relative rather than an absolute difference, cigarette smuggling being an example. Both parallel trade and transborder trade are parts of the more generic term of *smuggling*, which, as Andreas observes, is defined as "the practice of bringing in or taking out illicitly or by stealth."[70]

As regards illegal logging, the transborder trade in merbau provides a typical example, albeit atypical by its mere scale. The data are available from the excellent "undercover" work done by the London-based NGO, the Environmental Investigation Agency (EIA) and its partner, the NGO Telapak, based in Bogor, Java, Indonesia (see Table 3.6). Every month 300,000 m³ of merbau are smuggled out of Indonesia's Papua Province. The traffic involves middlemen in Jakarta, Singapore, and Hong Kong, but the product itself, the logs, is smuggled via Malaysia to the PRC. The product is smuggled out of Indonesia, where

Table 3.6 Merbau (*Intsia palembanica*) pricing structure

Phase of trade	US$/m³
Price paid to Papuan community	11
Price paid at point of export from Papua	120
Price of logs at entry to the PRC	240
Flooring price in the PRC	468
(1m³ provides 26m² of flooring)	
Flooring price in U.K. or U.S.A.	2288

Source: EIA and Telapak, *The Last Frontier: Illegal Logging in Papua and China's Massive Timber Theft* (London: EIA, February 2005), 27.

a ban of the exportation of logs has been in existence since October 2001, by means of corruption payments of $200,000 per shipment. In Malaysia, the product is issued with new (false) paperwork showing its origin as Malaysian. The product is then exported to the port of Shangjingang near Shanghai, from where it is transported overland to the city of Nanxun south of Shanghai. In Nanxun, 200 sawmills cut only merbau logs to provide flooring planks.

Alice Blondel notes that timber is a commodity which is easy to negotiate and trade, and which therefore has become of great interest to warring factions, organized crime, and arms dealers.[71] Arms dealers, be they individual businessmen, governments or quasi-governmental business entities, often trade in situations of direct or indirect barter; at the very least, they see natural resources as commodities providing their clients with the necessary funding for arms purchases.

An issue which has not attracted much attention is that of the armed militias employed by the timber companies. As funds originating from the forestry sector are used by local militias to purchase or barter weapons, in the same way such funds are used by timber companies to buy local armed militias. The trade in arms—and its relationship to illegal timber— is by its very nature secretive. A couple of the individuals involved in the traffic of direct or indirect barter of arms against timber have now become known to a wider public. The following paragraph examines one so-called "merchant of death." Although he is a substantial violator, it is not known if he is the biggest or, indeed, if he is typical.

Guus van Kouwenhoven, a Dutch businessman born in 1943, was close to former president of Liberia, Charles Taylor.[72] He was arrested in the Netherlands on 18 March 2005. Throughout the civil war, which raged for seven years in Liberia and caused the death of approximately 250,000 people, the parties to the conflict financed their war activities through overly exploiting and exporting the natural resources of the country. In particular, Charles Taylor used the funds generated by the excessive exploitation of timber and diamond extraction illegally to acquire large quantities of arms. In his position as Director of Operations of the Oriental Timber Company[73] and of the Royal Timber Company in Liberia, van Kouwenhoven managed the biggest timber operations in Liberia. Having very close relations with Charles Taylor, he facilitated the import of arms for the latter, thereby infringing resolutions of the UN Security Council.[74] The United Nations consequently issued an order in 2001 banning van Kouwenhoven from traveling, qualifying him as "an arms trafficker in breach of Resolution 1343 of the Security Council" in addition to being "someone who supported the efforts of ex-President Taylor in destabilizing Sierra

Leone to gain illegal access to its diamonds." As indicated above, this individual was arrested in the Netherlands in March 2005 in cooperation between the Special Court for Sierra Leone (SCSL), which had assisted Dutch investigators, and the Dutch authorities. In the case, in which he is a defendant, he seems to be accused of having delivered arms to Liberia in violation of UN sanctions and to be involved in war crimes committed in Liberia. The case also seems to deal with his relationship with and employment of militia groups, whose main activity was the security of his timber companies, but who as such became involved in the civil war which was then ravaging the country. According to the prosecution, "the militias hired by the former timber companies belonging to this Dutchman, are accused of participating in the massacre of civilians not even sparing the life of babies. Guus van Kouwenhoven is accused of having supplied the arms to the militias to enable them to carry out these crimes."[75] On 7 June 2006 in the Netherlands, he was sentenced to eight years' imprisonment for arms smuggling, but was not found guilty of war crimes. Both the public prosecutor and Kouwenhoven appealed the sentence.

The EIA (a renowned NGO) in 2008 estimated criminals' gains from illicit traffic in ivory, timber, and skins from protected animals at $10 billion. This traffic is highly organized and almost inevitably, international.

In this section on environmental crime, we noted among other things the relationship between deforestation and militia groups. It is intuitively clear that such relationships are even more ominous in the context of UN peace operations; the next section will examine this important, albeit often overlooked subject.

Peacekeeping and organized crime

Transnational organized crime—and organized crime in general—presents a particular set of problems in the context of peacekeeping missions. This section examines this special case in some detail, since the noxious effect in peacekeeping circumstances of organized crime, known in this respect as *a peace spoiler*, has been recognized by the United Nations. The High-level Panel Report, for instance, names transnational organized crime as one of the major threats to international stability.[76]

It is important, however, at the very outset, to underline that in this context, more than in any other, the remarks on taxonomy and identity in Chapter 1 are crucial: in sub-state conflictual situations identities become fluctuating and one player can, at the same time, fully claim several. He or she can for example concurrently be an ideological military combatant, organized crime figure, and politician.

Peacekeeping operations without exception take place in fragile and combat-ridden countries or regions characterized by a high-intensity level of violence, either in the present or in the immediate past. This has a number of consequences, the first and most important of which is often overlooked, *affective alienation*. It is, in general, part of our human make-up that witnessing, exercising, or being subjected to intense violence over a long period of time numbs us in our very humanity and, counter-intuitively, makes violence in some sense more acceptable. Second, combat brings poverty, misery, and illness (because of a breakdown in public hygiene) to many and—in particular in modern sub-state conflicts—riches (sometimes immense riches) and power to a few. And as studies on crime have shown, while poverty is not criminogenic, visible inequality is.[77]

Third, the presence of foreign troops, be they peacekeeping or combat troops, brings into the country foreign currency, trading opportunities, and new demands, in particular in the sex industry. Finally, a number of often charismatic, but always power-hungry and brutal individuals attempt to profit from the institutional frailty, be it temporary, surrounding them. In order to secure positions of power in the present unsettled circumstances as well as their political future, they need to build up—and therefore nourish—groups of individuals devoted to their person as opposed to an ideological program.

In this way, the scene is set for organized crime. Depending on the area of the world, foreign organized crime elements will presumably already have been attracted by the promise of easy gains, for example in countries rich in natural resources such as the Democratic Republic of Congo or Liberia, or countries that produce, or are important for the transit of, illicit goods, such as Afghanistan and the Balkans.

Case study: Chinese organized crime in Italy

For the student of transnational organized crime the implantation of Chinese organized crime in Italy, amidst some of the best organized, longest existing, and most determined organized crime groups in the world, cannot but offer a fruitful field of observation. Which arrangements will the various organizations establish? Will they carve up the territory along thematic lines with each group concentrating on a specific activity? Or are they going to exhaust each other in interminable crime warfare? Although much still is unclear, the answer to these questions is as fascinating as the questions, but, it is fair to say, more surprising. In fact, Chinese organized crime originates in a totally different socio-political, non-contiguous environment, with appreciable difficulties in learning a foreign and to them totally unrelated language (including in this context several important dialects). While they themselves represented a closed, impenetrable criminal management environment and faced a criminal culture equally characterized by a mental and social walled-in mentality, yet they nevertheless achieved the unachievable. Although initially some observers opined that Chinese organized crime would be submitted to the so-called *pizzo* (Italian slang for the payment of "protection money"), it soon became clear that Chinese organized crime not only had achieved a peace agreement with the major Italian criminal organizations, but they had identified mutual complementarities, which will be treated below. Chinese organized crime, however, was able concurrently also to elaborate agreements with another recent immigrant crime organization in Italy, Nigerian crime groups.

Chinese organized crime has as one of its main sources of income the retail sale of counterfeit products, from counterfeit luxury goods to aircraft spare parts as well as of product which is not licensed for sale on the European markets because of health concerns, such as toys. This poses a serious problem since such product is very bulky when compared with other illicit goods, for example drugs. I would argue that this is exactly where Chinese organized crime identified important complementarities with Italian organized crime. The former could produce, ship, and distribute the various products, but the latter could ensure the goods' entry into the territory of Italy—and therefore of the European Union—since Italian organized crime, the Camorra and the 'ndrangheta in particular, have an established network based on Italy's ports, which they in some sense "control."

As of 1 January 2007, there were 144,886 legal Chinese immigrants in Italy;[78] the number of illegal immigrants obviously remains unknown, although at least one scholar, Maria Laura Iacobone, estimates that there are 2–3 illegal immigrants for each legal one.[79] As in other relevant examples, for instance the Italian immigration into the United States in the last century, Chinese organized crime arrived along with the immigrants, as a natural, indistinguishable part of them, but also ready to exploit the fragile situation, in which all newly arrived and not well integrated immigrants find themselves. With the benefit of hindsight, it is now clear that Chinese organized crime in Italy found not only a congenial criminal environment in which and with which to operate, but also a bridgehead from which to organize extensive illegal activities in European markets. These main activities involve trafficking in waste, counterfeit cigarettes, counterfeit luxury products, and humans for prostitution and for labor, as well as immigrant smuggling and money laundering. Some observers opine that Italy was chosen as a bridgehead because it is "the country of corruption."[80] Whether corruption in Italy is widespread will not be considered here, but I would argue that, counter-intuitively, Chinese organized crime chose Italy because of the presence of very well-established endogenous crime organizations, which they correctly saw not as competitors, but as potential associates.

The profits accruing to Chinese organized crime in Italy is estimated at 1 billion euros a year.

Counterfeit cigarettes

In the 1980s and 1990s, the Camorra and Albanian organized crime smuggled genuine cigarettes from the Balkan countries into Italy. Since these cigarettes did not carry the Italian tax stickers proving that the appropriate taxes had been paid, they had to be sold on the black market at discounted prices. Now, however, Chinese in cooperation with Italian organized crime earn the total wholesale price in profit. Since both cigarettes and tax stickers are counterfeit they can be sold through the usual tobacconist outlets at market price, whereas product costs are negligible. The following paragraphs contain a couple of examples of recent seizures in order to illustrate the scope of the traffic.

On 9 May 2008 in Naples, Italian authorities seized eight tons of counterfeit Marlboro and Marlboro Light cigarettes, constituted by 39,150 cartons or 7,830,000 cigarettes.[81] The counterfeit cigarettes, which originated in China, carried counterfeit Italian tax stickers and, therefore, were destined for the Italian market, where they would have fetched close to €1,700,000, of which €1,350,000 would have constituted non-paid government taxes that instead accrued to organized crime.[82] In Sicily in the six months ending May 2008, 20 million Chinese (counterfeit) cigarettes were seized, while in November 2007, in Ancona, on Italy's Adriatic coast, the authorities seized 40 tons of counterfeit cigarettes, or 40 million cigarettes.

Italy, however, is also used by Chinese organized crime as a transit point for counterfeit cigarettes destined for countries outside of the European Union. Thus, in Cagliari, Sardinia, in December 2007, €5 million worth of counterfeit cigarettes (20 million cigarettes) were seized en route for Togo and Benin.[83]

Waste management

Both scholars and law enforcement consider waste management, in particular that of toxic waste, the future gateway to substantial profits for organized crime and, again, Chinese and Italian organized crime have identified a series of complementarities. To understand the involvement of organized crime in this surprising traffic in waste, one needs to consider that the legal destruction of dangerous waste of one twenty-foot container costs €60,000; the corresponding illegal elimination is €5,000 in the Far East.[84] Entities that generate substantial quantities of waste, mostly manufacturing companies, but also hospitals, over the last 10 years or so have therefore contracted directly with Italian organized crime or with convenient cover companies for organized crime to dispose of the waste generated. Hitherto, organized crime has used landfills and naturally occurring cavities to dispose of the waste.[85] Now, however, the natural grottos of Campania are full; and China is the alternative. Italian organized crime has therefore allied itself with Chinese organized crime and ships the waste to China, where it is dumped in coastal villages, the inhabitants of which—unaware of any danger inherent in the toxicity of some of the material—attempt to recuperate as much material as possible. Interestingly—and perhaps worryingly—parts of the illegal waste shipped to China are returned to Italy for reuse as plastic raw material or to be formed into plastic objects. In this way, plastic from illegal waste from hospitals is reused in toys and spectacles. The following paragraph highlights a number of recent seizures.

In 2006, 9,000 tons of toxic waste in 286 containers destined for exportation were seized by Italian customs, most of it en route for China[86] and in the so-called "Operation Great Wall", from November 2005 to June 2006, authorities in Reggio Calabria in southern Italy, in an operation which involved waste from 23 Italian companies, seized 135 containers of 740 tons of plastic, 1,570 tons of metal, 150 tons of used electrical instruments, 700 tons of paper waste, and 10 tons of used car parts and tires, en route for China, India, Russia, and North Africa.[87]

Human trafficking

Chinese organized crime in Italy is heavily involved in the trafficking in humans, who, on the last leg of their journey—depending on costs they are willing to sustain—enter Italy either by being smuggled by boat from the Balkans across the Adriatic Sea or concealed in trucks crossing the northeastern border at Trieste, or by air displaying counterfeit passports, which allow them to pose as Korean tourists. In the very rare cases where the smuggled person has been able to pay the cost immediately (up to $30,000 if by air), he or she is now free to commence his or her life as a clandestine immigrant. In the vast majority of cases, however, the principle of indenture obtains, whereby the cost of transportation is transformed into a debt that the smuggled person owes the criminal organization, and which he or she has to work off, by working in sweatshops or by prostitution. For the sake of brevity only prostitution will be considered here.

In this area, Chinese organized crime uses women who have been smuggled from China and who in difficult circumstances work off their debt to the smuggler. Contrary to Albanian and Nigerian organized crime, whose prostitutes operate on the streets, Chinese organized crime prostitutes work out of apartments. They can expect to earn €3,000 a day (€100–300 per client according to requirements). They work two weeks in one location before being moved to a new one, partly to avoid them becoming too familiar with the location and its customer base, partly to be able continually to offer new choices to customers. The women are released once they have paid off their indenture. Attempts to escape, or reporting to local authorities, are punished severely—if necessary by punishing the woman's family left behind in China—and even suicide reportedly is not a solution, since the debt incurred is simply transferred to the dead woman's family in China.

Money laundering

Chinese organized crime learnt from one of the three main Italian criminal organizations, the 'ndrangheta, the technique of purchasing shops, in which they sell various goods, in particular women's fashion, that few or nobody would want to buy; the purpose of the shops is not commerce, but the generation of general sales receipts for non-existing sales in order to launder illicit gains.

The remittances sent to Zehjiang prefecture in China in general and to the city of Wenzhou in particular are surprising considering the number of Chinese immigrants in Italy. The vast majority of remittances are effectuated via money transfer agencies (such as Western Union), notwithstanding the fact that such agencies charge higher fees than banks. The operations, which are always in cash and at €12,000–12,500, just below the reporting requirement of anti-money laundering (AML) regulations, are almost all thought to be funds of illicit origin. By way of an example, one such money transfer agency in 2007 transferred €500 million to China.[88]

In January 2008, Italian authorities charged 12 Italians and 6 Chinese with having established an illegal bank, including a number of branch offices, each of which transferred €1,000,000 every working day. The banks' clients all had extensive criminal records for counterfeiting, smuggling, and tax evasion.

The organizations

Italian authorities have had difficulties in investigating and prosecuting Chinese organized crime, for three main reasons. First, the well established impenetrability of the Chinese milieu makes it difficult for investigators to obtain information. Not only are Chinese immigrant communities in themselves closed for linguistic and socio-cultural reasons, but this is aggravated by the fact that immigration follows regional patterns, so that a majority of immigrants in a certain country originate from the same region in China and, as regards the organized crime elements in the community, these will often be from the same town and a large part of them known to each other either directly or through family recommendations.

The immigrant society thereby becomes very tight-knit, and any attempt by the law enforcement authorities of establishing an undercover operation inconceivable. Second, one encounters severe problems with translation of Chinese dialects used. This is obviously of importance during interrogations, but even more so when related to telephone intercepts. To this should be added the fact that while it is relatively easy to find trustworthy interpreters in the best known dialects, Cantonese and Mandarin, it is practically impossible to find interpreters that can be trusted in the lesser known dialects (unfortunately those mostly spoken by Chinese criminals) of Hokkien, Teochew, and Hakka. Finally, Chinese immigrants display a reluctance to give testimony, which is mostly based on fear, caused for example by the savage killings of witnesses against the Hsiang family in Tuscany,[89] but also because of a clear feeling of belonging to a separate community, which does not interact with "the white man," disdainfully referred to as *kuailo* (Cantonese for "foreign devil"). There is a parallel here with the traditional Sicilian Mafioso as the man who can take care of himself.

The ability of Chinese organized crime to integrate and cooperate with criminals from a different culture is not confined to the example of Italy. The Russian Far East is now a major area of expansion for Chinese organized crime. Indeed, some 10 years ago Vladivostok was controlled by Russian crime bosses, and drive-by shootings, kidnappings, etc., were not unusual. This is no longer the case. As Bertil Lintner expresses it, the Russian bosses are out and the Triads are in; the latter being much more sophisticated than the Russians they have replaced, street crime has disappeared: "they view public disorder as a threat to their criminal enterprises." The remarkable fact to observe, however, is that Chinese organized crime has been able to incorporate or integrate many of the lower-level Russian criminals and ensure that they accept the Chinese "way of doing business."[90]

Case study: Operation Green Quest

This case study was chosen for its illustrative qualities.[91] The case covers the whole spectrum of criminal activities, from the most uncompli-cated, retail theft, to the more complicated, international money laun-dering and, almost certainly, the financing of terrorism, while including also the attempted use of professional assassins in order to neutralize the lead investigative officials, and the use of businesses and the falsi-fication of business records in the execution of the criminal enterprise. Although the investigation of the crime commenced in September 2001 in Texas, and those responsible have been sentenced and incarcerated, the "criminal model" has spread throughout the United States. In fact, the spatio-temporal implications of the case have not been fully understood by U.S. prosecutorial authorities, who realize neither the extent in time and space of the modus operandi nor the impact of the same on the rather nebulous concept of the financing of terrorism.

The specific investigation considered in this subsection concerns a criminal organization known as the Ghali organization from the name of the lead member, which was active in the state of Texas, and con-sisted of persons mostly of Middle Eastern descent. They recruited hundreds of shoplifters, drug addicts, and other marginalized persons to engage in a variety of criminal activities in order to obtain the higher-value products typically sold in an American convenience store, inter alia over-the-counter (OTC) medicinal products, infant formula, diabetes test strips, razors, and pregnancy test kits, acting in their choice of products in accordance with instructions received from the organization. The street level criminals used a variety of methods to obtain such products in high volume: They would fill a shopping trol-ley with the merchandise, pretend to approach the check-out positions near the exit, and then race the cart out of the exit and up into the back of a waiting van. Also armed robberies and warehouse thefts were used, as well as counterfeit merchandising coupons, counterfeit Women, Infants and Children (WIC) coupons, and food stamp fraud. The stolen and fraudulently obtained goods were aggregated in ware-houses belonging to the Ghali organization, where security tags and price stickers were removed. False accounting entries were made in the Ghali organization's company books in order to "legitimize" the origin of the products, which in bi-weekly, interstate shipments were then sold to wholesalers, some of whom were aware of the origin of the goods, some of whom were not.

The resultant profits were regularly deposited in the organization's bank accounts. Some of the proceeds were employed to buy residences in Texas, while the rest were transformed into banker's checks and hand-carried, concealed by a variety of methods, to Amman, Jordan, where the proceeds, at least in part, were invested in real estate. The final destination of the funds that were successfully transferred to the Middle East is under investigation by the appropriate security services; it would be unhelpful to examine that final leg of the criminal enterprise at this time, although the implications of the transfers and the interest of mentioned security services are self-evident. It can be noted that several Middle Eastern individuals who conducted business with the Ghali organization have suspected terrorism links. One of Ghali's associates was the target of a Foreign Intelligence Surveillance Act (FISA) wiretap and subsequently indicted on a variety of criminal charges, while another reportedly smuggled $78 million to Palestine and fled the United States. The illegal proceeds derived from the same modus operandi as that used by the Ghali organization.

Ali Alidimi, another Ghali associate, pled guilty to federal charges and agreed to the forfeiture of approximately $800,000 in illegal proceeds that were seized in 1999 by federal agents. The currency was discovered by agents when Alidimi attempted to ship the money to Yemen concealed in hair dye boxes. Federal investigators allege that Alidimi has known ties to Hamas and was involved in terrorist financing.

In 1999, U.S. customs and the Fort Worth Police Department arrested and indicted several members of the so-called Saadat organization for trafficking in counterfeit goods and money laundering. One of the members of the Saadat family, by his own admission, had been trained in a Bin Laden terrorist camp.

Mohammed Khalil Ghali was convicted in April 2005 in Dallas, Texas, to 14 years imprisonment: Conspiracy (one count), 60 months; theft (one count), 120 months; money laundering (nine counts), 168 months; plus three counts of interstate transportation of stolen goods.[92]

One may note, with concern, that prosecution concentrated on, and obtained the heaviest custodial sentence for, the money laundering charges and not on the predicate, very serious organized crime offences. It is perhaps judicially expedient to sanction the money laundering aspects of a case more severely than the underlying criminality, yet I would argue that such an approach to criminal justice undermines the societal consent, which condemns the crime itself rather than the subsequent movements of the proceeds from this, and thus exsanguinates the universal condemnation of the crime, without which criminal jurisdiction has little meaning.

Although interesting in and by itself, the case is only fully to be understood when seen in its larger context. In a conversation with one of the two lead investigators, the author was informed that the modus operandi had been known to him for more than twenty year.[93] Persons of Middle Eastern origin[94] set up small convenience stores in low-income urban areas; the start-up capital, also known as "seed money," to the best of his knowledge, was provided by Hamas and Hezbollah operatives. Being in a low-income area, the convenience store owners then made it known that they were in the market for product "of whatever origin." After consolidation, goods would then be shipped in interstate commerce to wholesalers or retailers. A part of the resultant profits would be shipped to the Middle East, more often than not to Amman, Jordan. Not only is this modus operandi known to have been going on in Texas; similar groups using similar methods are active in Utah, California, Florida, and other states of the U.S.A.

The modus operandi of the Ghali organization is of crucial interest to students of organized crime, since the organization retained its character of an institution through the years, even when individuals changed. An obvious question which comes to mind, is: Why is not an end brought to the existence of the organization and its modus operandi, considering that it is built on flagrant criminality? The answer presumably has many facets. First, looked at from the local prosecutorial level, the individual cases are small. Second, this modus operandi is an example of not being able to see the local and the global at the same time—see the discussion of scaling theory in the Introduction. U.S. Attorneys at the local level cannot make the not obvious, but very real, connection between a small retail theft or retail fencing offence and the financing behind, say, a major international terrorist attack or the funding of the successful Hezbollah resistance to the Israeli army in the course of the 2006 Israeli invasion of Lebanon. Elsewhere throughout this work, it has been stressed that the inability of decision makers as well as of analysts to perceive the totality of a network of individuals and their actions severely limits both our conceptualization of organized crime and, indeed, of the relationship between organized crime and globalization.

Third, although economists have proven that an illicit market has never been defeated from the supply side, a large part of U.S.—and indeed other countries'—drug law enforcement is concentrated on the supply side, crop eradication, drug interception overseas, etc. This irrational approach presumably covers two major defaults, political expediency and pride. As pointed out above, it is politically expedient to perceive all imperfections as exogenous. In the present context, it is politically more acceptable to see terrorism financing as an activity undertaken "overseas" in order for foreigners to perform terrorist acts "here," rather than to acknowledge that major parts of the flows are quite the reverse, namely funds generated in the West, by nationals or immigrants who allegedly have been successfully integrated into the host culture, and transferred overseas to finance violent acts in foreign jurisdictions.

Fourth, the role of the diaspora populations should be noted, albeit not exaggerated: "Collecting funds from the diaspora, although a long-standing practice, has become a significant source of financing. The Irish Republican Army (IRA) has drawn a large part of its revenues from the Irish community in the United States, and this has also been done by the Armed Islamic Group (GIA) in Algeria, by the Al-Qaeda, Sri Lankan rebels, Armenian terrorists … "[95]

The modus operandi continues, however, and on 31 May 2007 in the U.S. District Court, Louisville, Kentucky, a federal jury found one Eyad Suleiman, a.k.a. Abu Zacheria, guilty of knowingly receiving and possessing stolen OTC pharmaceuticals. Again, the quantities involved were considerable: One of his former employees testified that in an eight-month period in 2005, Suleiman sold over 6 million dollars worth of stolen pharmaceuticals, which he had purchased for 4 million dollars. Another witness explained that people walked in from the street and sold OTC pharmaceuticals to Suleiman for approximately one-third of retail price. She herself, on any given day, would steal $10–20,000 of OTC pharmaceuticals and sell them to Suleiman. An accomplice was charged with laundering of $70 million in checks, which he cashed for Suleiman.[96] A representative from the Organized Retail Crime Division Coordinator for Walgreens Corporation testified that this type of theft costs Walgreens approximately $700 million per year throughout the United States and that organized shoplifting in general costs retail business in the United States $34 billion per year.[97]

It is, unfortunately, clear that this modus operandi continues throughout the United States and perhaps elsewhere in the world. This situation underlines two points: first, the fact that we need to consider the possibility that terrorism, including the maintenance of a small army under arms, is funded by many distinct, small, but constantly spouting taps rather than from massive transfers of funds; and second, the need for national, regional, and international law enforcement intelligence cooperation. In fact, from an intelligence point of view, this case demonstrates the scaling theory rather well; looked at in detail, as above, one comprehends the working of the criminal organization at local level; however, only by looking at it from afar can one develop enough of a macro-view to be able to appreciate the operation in its entirety, and to comprehend the magnitude and ultimate purpose of many disparate, seemingly irrelevant or minor facts.

Concurrently, Operation Green Quest presents the scholar with an important insight into the concept of *identity*, which might very well be a constituent part of organized crime. In investigating the issue of organized retail theft in the state of Texas, the investigators disclosed that the particular organization of the crime had barely changed over twenty years. The major commodities targeted had changed, from cigarettes to baby formula and similar high-priced items, the players—both the street-level thieves and robbers and the organizers, acting as wholesalers for the illegally obtained goods—had all changed, but "the organization" remained. The changes have obviously been very slow with one commodity being replaced by another and one player with another, but in the end everything has changed, while everything has remained the same. That, in fact, might very well be the core characteristic which distinguishes "organized crime" from criminality that has been organized (gangs). One cannot but be reminded of the words of Tancredi in Tomasi di Lampedusa's *Il Gattopardo* (1958): *Se vogliamo che tutto rimanga com'è, bisogna che tutto cambi* ("If we want everything to remain the same, everything must change").[98]

This chapter has provided a rather wide overview of some of the more important activities of transnational organized crime, and in particular it has studied at some length the implantation of one criminal organization in the territory of another and their horizontal, almost seamless cooperation. The case study which rounds off the chapter touched on the relationship between organized crime and terrorism; this subject will be further explored in the following chapter.

4 Transnational crime and terrorism

This chapter examines the possible interrelationship between terrorism and transnational organized crime, and it questions the conceptual paradigms presently used in scholarly research of this area. Writings in the area of terrorism are, almost inevitably, based on the latest known variety of the crime. Post-9/11, the—vastly prevalent—terrorism concept is that of religion-based activities originating in the Middle East. This, however, neglects for example the endogenous terrorism of 1970s Europe, the Acah terrorism in Indonesia, and the various terrorist groupings concentrating on the Kashmir question.

A proposed definition of terrorism

In Chapter 1 of this work, I argue that we will never be able to further studies into the nebulous area of organized crime without adopting the kind of differential diagnosis methodology used in medicine; similarly, we will not advance understanding in terrorism studies—and in the studies of the interaction between organized crime and terrorism—without adopting much more precise conceptual tools than those presently available.

The intensification of interest in terrorism at the beginning of the twenty-first century, in particular as a result of the two terrorist attacks perpetrated in the heart of the Western economic centers, "9/11" (11 September 2001, New York) and "7/7" (7 July 2005, London) has, quite understandably, led to the question of whether or not there is a relation, operational or conceptual, between organized crime and terrorism.[1] Terrorism, like organized crime but even more so, because of the political and emotional undertones that pervade it, has not been defined, be it on international or national level. For instance, the United Nations agreed to disagree and instead adopted a thematic approach; only the 1977 European Convention on the Suppression of Terrorism was nonthematic.[2] The latter also acknowledges the difficulties caused by the so-called "political exception" rule and stipulates six types of terrorist act which cannot be regarded as political offenses.

In order to collocate the differential understanding of terrorism within observable parameters and to further refine the conceptual tools available, I propose the following definition:[3]

> Terrorism is the triangular and communicative use by one or more sub-state actors of illegal acts of violence: the originator (the terrorist) sends a message via the transmitter (the victim) to the receiver (an authority) with a view to influence the outcome of the latter's administrative, judicial or political processes and, by showing the weaknesses of the latter, to evince to a fourth party, the people represented by the media, the necessity for political change.

A well-formed quip, "Few die, many watch," adequately sums up this tragic triangle. This view of terrorism excludes the use of the term to cover so-called "state terror," since this term is used by contemporary scholarship in many senses that are not necessarily made explicit. For example, a ruler's use of terror on their own population to impose his or her will is not considered terrorism on this view, since it is not triangular and the message is not aimed at an authority. The ruler's acts do install *terror* in the population, but from a taxonomical point of view it makes more sense to view such acts as excessive coercion. This type of terror, which is a resultant, not a technique or tactic, would not meet the criteria of the Bruce Hoffman definition, either, since its aim is not political change, rather the opposite. Likewise, the term is often taken to mean a state using its own agents to perpetrate acts of violence in another state or funding charitable or political organizations that it knows engage in terrorism or in the funding of terrorism. In both cases, I maintain that it would be more helpful to see the state in question as engaging in covert warfare, in the former directly by the use of its own agents, and in the latter indirectly, by the use of interposed agents.

The definition proposed here quite obviously concentrates on *propositional terrorism*, which consists in installing terror into a population in order to make a statement, a proposition. This leads one to consider the concept of *speech act*, which, in the context of terrorism, means the total communicational image emanating from the terrorist or terrorist group, including the terrorist acts themselves, the writings of the groups, their slogans and graffiti; even their occasional silence is part of the speech act. To use a term from John Austin, the terrorist speech act is *performative*, that is "both saying and doing something"; it is, however, *disguised performative*.[4]

Finally, one needs to contemplate the purpose of such terrorism, which, following Baroness O'Neill, I argue, is *the creation of uncertainty in the community*,[5] not only in the sense of fear ("where will they hit next?") but, much more importantly, in making the population reconsider what can be termed "cherished values," including a certain notion of what constitutes acceptable criminal justice procedures. Therefore, a government which reacts to terrorism by imposing hitherto unacceptable criminal justice measures, such as extensive violation of the right to privacy, for instance in telecommunications or in conducting business, or by authorizing prolonged pre-trial detention without court order, plays into the hands of terrorists by creating the kind of polarized, quasi-militarized society that fundamentally destroys society as it was and, indeed, as it was "cherished." This, in a sense, has been exactly the goal of the terrorists.

Terrorists and organized criminals: birds of a feather?

Terrorism and organized crime have little in common on an intellectual level, since the former is based on ideological, religious or political principles, while the latter on profit motives. It is clear, nevertheless, that one illegal actor may use the methodology of the other, so that terrorists will engage in common and organized crime, typically armed robbery, extortion, criminal abduction, or drug trafficking, to fund their operations, while organized crime may use terrorist methodology to "send messages." Furthermore, terrorists and organized criminals may cooperate, as is the case in Colombia, where a terrorist group, the Revolutionary Armed Forces of Colombia (FARC), against remuneration protects drug convoys. Other similar examples are provided by the Liberation Tigers of Tamil Eelam (LTTE) in Sri Lanka, the Kurdistan Workers Party (PKK) in Turkey, and various factions in Somalia and the Russian Caucasus. Likewise, according to some scholars, the infrastructures in Lebanon of the Popular Front for the Liberation of Palestine (PFLP)[6] are being used for the transfer of narcotic drugs to the West. The clear advantage to the terrorist group is that it obtains a stable means of funding and no longer has to rely on the vicissitudes of sponsorship.[7] Some terrorist groups, however, slowly permute from being politically motivated to simply being criminal organizations. Many scholars claim that such is the case for the IRA in Northern Ireland, which started out being involved in a number of smaller rackets from the 1980s until, according to most experts, it became a purely criminal organization.[8]

The crime-terror continuum

The area has been extensively and impressively studied by the scholar Tamara Makarenko, who proposes the so-called "crime-terror continuum," which will be treated at some length in this subsection.[9] The end of the Cold War also brought an end to or at least severely curtailed state sponsorship of civil wars, insurgencies, and terrorism. Terrorists—and, indeed, civil war parties and insurgency groups—therefore had to seek funding elsewhere. Civil wars became natural resource centered, as both parties in a conflict sought to control such resources, and therefore funding, whereas terrorist groups turned to the domain which hitherto had been reserved for organized crime. There had, of course, been a precedent in so-called narco-terrorism in Latin and South America—see below. The increased exploitation of criminality by terrorists was facilitated by a number of relatively new phenomena, linked to the globalization of our societies, namely the remarkable expansion in international trade, travel, and communications. The point here is not only that such international activities became gradually less burdensome and less expensive. Rather, that the sheer volume made illicit international trade, travel, etc., much more difficult to identify among the licit activities.

The whole spectrum or continuum can, however, best be illustrated graphically, in Figure 4.1, by what is referred to as the Makarenko scale.

The scale can be read from left to right and from right to left and consists of four groups: alliances (point 1), operational motivations (point 2), convergence (point 3), and the "black hole" (point 4).

At the lowest level, the nexus between transnational organized crime and terrorism consists in one using the methodology of the other, also

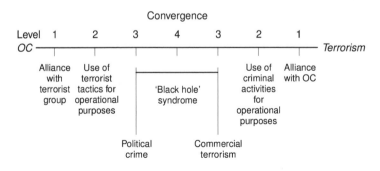

Figure 4.1 The crime-terror continuum
Source: Tamara Makarenko, "The crime-terror continuum: Tracing the interplay between transnational organised crime and terrorism," *Global Crime* 6, no. 1 (2004): 129–45, at 131.

known as *activity appropriation*, most commonly seen in the use by terrorist organizations of criminality in order to further their political aims by terrorism. On a slightly higher level, point 1 on the Makarenko scale is the *alliance*, whereby one group buys in knowledge from the other; typically, the terrorist group will acquire, for example, false passports from organized crime; and organized crime might require knowledge of explosives from terrorists. Apart from access to the particular expertise, both parties have advantages: transnational organized crime operates better in an environment of uncertainty, where the institutions are destabilized, while the activities of organized crime further install in the population a feeling of helplessness, of governmental failure, etc., which is beneficial to the purposes of the terrorist cause. It is quite obvious, however, that on the level of alliances, both groups also expose themselves to serious security risks, both because the circle of people with knowledge of the criminal acts expands and because there is no real level of trust between the two parties in the alliance. Therefore, both groups will rather avoid buying in expertise and will instead attempt to incorporate such knowledge within their own group, in order to "ensure organizational security."[10]

When both groups have acquired the various in-house expertise needed and alliances are no longer necessary nor, indeed, desirable, one moves to point 2 on the Makarenko scale, where organized crime uses terrorist tactics to influence operational conditions, while terrorists engage in organized crime—also for operational purposes—to acquire the necessary funding.

Once one moves one step further on the scale, one enters the area of *convergence*, where, at point 3 on the scale, one needs to remain focused on the "operational motivation," by which, at least initially as one moves toward the center, the groups are differentiated, depending on whether they originate on the left- or right-hand side of the scale. At this point of their taxonomical development, criminal groups apply terrorist means and engage in political activity in order to influence the institutional environment, whereas terrorists apply criminal means in order to replace the funding from state sponsors lost at the end of the Cold War. In this middle area, so-called convergence has been completed and one enters into an area where the two organizations have converged into "a single entity that initially displays the characteristics of both groups simultaneously."[11] By so-called *transformation*, a group in this middle area might develop further along the scale in the same direction and end up on the side of the scale opposite to the one from where it originated. Transformation occurs when it is the case "that the ultimate aims and motivations of the organization have actually changed. In these cases, the groups no longer retain the defining points that had hitherto made them a political or criminal group."[12] The cases discussed under this heading concern either a criminal group displaying political motivations or a terrorist group, which slowly begins to use its political rhetoric as a facade solely for perpetrating criminal activities. In the latter case, one typically sees a terrorist group, which initially obtains funding through criminal activity and uses such funds for political activity, but then slowly commences to divert more and more of the funds into personal consumption. The former case concerns criminal organizations, which initially have applied terrorist means to influence, say, on carceral procedures, but then slowly attempt to gain political control and control over the institutions; or who initially have used terrorism to establish a monopoly, territorial or in a particular business, or—more insidiously—over strategic natural resources, but then proceed to attempt to control the state itself.

It is worth noting that the Mafia bombings of popular tourist locations in Italy such as the Uffizi in Florence and the San Giovanni in Laterano church in Rome backfired. Far from leading to institutional disarray, they helped create a unified, firm front against the Mafia. The latter almost immediately understood its strategic error and decided to discontinue the use of such means. Organized crime has been more successful in the use of selective assassinations of judges, law enforcement personnel, and, indeed, other government officials, which, quite understandably, creates a certain amount of institutional disquiet, as did for example the killings of high-ranking anti-drug enforcement officials in Mexico in May 2008.

At the very midpoint of the Makarenko scale, point 4, one finds the so-called "black hole syndrome," that is to say states that have become so weakened from a governance point of view that they ultimately generate safe havens for the operations of convergent groups. In other words, these are states where groups participating in a civil war set out with political motives, but then they develop a focus on criminal gains (so-called "decadent guerrillas," according to Paul Wilkinson[13]), or states that have been taken over by hybrid groups, which, according to Ralf Mutschke,[14] are groups whose political and criminal activities are deeply intertwined.

The methods and motives study

A U.S. government-funded study examined the link between terrorism and organized crime in considerable detail.[15] Although one might disagree with certain conceptual premises of the report, it nevertheless constitutes the most thorough government-sponsored treatment of the area to date. The report first deals with the concept of *activity appropriation*, which covers the very common situation where organized crime uses the methods of terrorism, or vice versa. It then identifies five different stages in the terror-crime interrelationship and refers to this linear scale as *the terror-crime interaction spectrum*. The first stage is termed *nexus*, which simply describes the possible business relationship, whereby one group "outsources" an activity such as the production of false passports, rather than internalizing the necessary expertise. The next step on the scale is *activity appropriation*, referred to above, followed by *the hybrid group*, a term used to describe a group, wherein "organized crime and terrorism are more or less equally important to the group." Somewhat incongruously, the authors continue by stating that the group "after all often needs to commit fraud, extortion and other staple activities of organized crime in order to fund its terror operations," whereby they throw serious doubt on their previous statement that organized crime and terrorism are more or less equally important to the group. If a hybrid group becomes so fixated on one activity that it drops the other, the change is termed *transformation*.[16]

The report quite rightly points to the prison as the environment where incarcerated criminals are converted to radicalized views. Thereby, a terrorist group will have gained not only a new proselyte, but also someone who can assist fundraising via his criminal activities, once released. This quite obviously leads one to question the concept of *identity*. The authors of the U.S. report claim that "Terrorists in European prisons recruit criminals to their cause, allowing incarcerated individuals to move between their identities as terrorists and criminals;" this, however, is a questionable view, which logically would only be true if one could only be one or the other, and if the two identities were exclusive. One may, however, very well be terrorist and shoe salesman at the same time and apply some of one's income from the shoe business to one's terrorist activities; it is difficult to see, why this should be fundamentally different if one habitually gains one's income from criminality. One does not switch from one identity to the other; one *is* both at the same time.[17]

Case study: funding of Jihad network by crime

In the night of 14–15 December 2005, French law enforcement executed a search warrant on a garage in a Parisian suburb. They seized 1 kg of military-type (C-4) explosives, 16 sticks of dynamite and 2 automatic weapons, 3 revolvers, ski-masks, bullet-proof vests, and a police uniform. The search was the result of the arrest, a couple of days prior, of almost a dozen individuals. The group was specialized in robberies and consisted of a number of rather heterogeneous individuals; one was a criminal well known for armed robbery and drug trafficking (Ben Hadj), and another a mathematician obsessed with international Jihad (Cherifi). The latter had previously been arrested in France, in August 2000, when he took possession of four false passports (made in Thailand), on which occasion he was sentenced to five years' imprisonment. At the time of his arrest, he frequented the milieus in London where al-Qaeda actively recruited for Afghanistan; to his regret he was rejected because of diabetes. While in prison, he encountered and converted Ben Hadj to a form of radical Islam.

A so-called salafist,[18] Majrar, a Moroccan national who had been expelled to Morocco from Greece, where he tried to enter on a false passport, had also known Cherifi in prison in France. He travelled incessantly between Egypt, Syria, and Turkey. He was interviewed in prison in Morocco and provided information on the group in France. This information and concurrent investigation in France disclosed that the purpose of the group was to raise funds to finance Jihad in Europe, and Cherifi had the added responsibility of recruiting suitable individuals for Iraq. The explosives, of which some had been used for a prior attempt to gain entry to the funds depot of a private security company, Securitas, in France, had been obtained from a Yugoslav national.[19]

This case study from France was chosen because it, interestingly, highlights the following issues, which are of universal import, but only when applied to Middle Eastern terrorism; they do not apply for example to the kind of endogenous terrorism, which obtained in Western Europe in the 1970s: Conversion and recruitment in prison; international contacts, namely passports from Thailand, explosive from a Yugoslav individual, travel to, spiritual inspiration from, and close contact with al-Qaeda operatives in the United Kingdom, and contacts, via Majrar, with Turkey, Syria, and Egypt; and financing of European Jihad network by organized crime-type activities

Narco-terrorism

The use of criminal methodology by terrorist groups and even such groups' eventual permutation into organized criminality should not be confounded with so-called *narco-terrorism*. This term is most commonly defined, as by Emmanuela Mylonaki, "activities initiated by drug traffickers using violence against individuals, property, a state or its agents, to intimidate and coerce people into modifying their actions in ways advantageous to the drug traffickers."[20] In other words, the term is used about a sub-group of organized crime, narcotic drug traffickers, who use terrorist means as part of their efforts to secure their criminal activities and profits—as a parallel to terrorists, who may use typical organized crime activities as part of their overall activities as terrorists. Scholars have also pointed out that organized crime has an interest in working with terrorists, inter alia since this renders extradition so much more complicated because of the "political offence" concept; terrorists, on the other hand, profit from the instability created by organized crime, since this diminishes the authority of the government and of the state.[21]

The term *narco-terrorism* might make sense, since it clearly fits into the definition proposed above, as well as into definitions elaborated by other scholars, the most widely used of which is by Bruce Hoffman, who defines terrorism as "The deliberate creation and exploitation of fear through violence or the threat of violence in the pursuit of political change," while the United States, in its criminal code, has codified terrorism as "The premeditated, politically motivated violence against noncombatant targets by sub-national groups or clandestine agents. International terrorism involves citizens, or territory, of more than one country. A terrorist group is any group practicing, or that has significant sub-groups that practice, international terrorism."[22] Nevertheless, other similar terminological compounds coined on the same cobbler's last, such as *eco-terrorism* and *cyber-terrorism*, are not helpful. Whatever crimes may hide under these denominations, they should not be denominated "terrorism" as they do not employ violence or the threat of violence to influence an authority's decision-making and thereby, ultimately, provoke political change.

A pragmatic example of the use by organized crime of terrorist methodology is provided by the so-called Sinaloa cartel in Mexico, a drug smuggling cartel. Whenever the federal authorities of Mexico take rigorous action against this cartel in its heartland on the Pacific coast, it retaliates by terrorist-type attacks against judges, law enforcement and other government officials in the country's capital, Mexico City. On 22 January 2008, 11 members of the cartel were arrested in two houses in Mexico City in possession of a large stockpile of explosives and automatic weapons; they were divided into three commando units and were reportedly preparing such terrorist-type violence. At the beginning of May 2008, the Sinaloa cartel assassinated five high-ranking Mexican police officials in one week in a clear terrorist-type message to the president of Mexico, who had strongly encouraged and supported an intensive anti-drug trafficking effort in the country.[23] That this strategy undoubtedly has had some effect in Mexico is proved by the resignation of ranking police officials, some of whom are demanding asylum abroad.[24] It can be argued that this use of terrorist means by organized crime (point 2 or perhaps point 3 on the left hand side of the Makarenko scale) has led to the institutional uncertainty desired by the drug traffickers.

The Mexican cartels furthermore provide an example of the way organized crime can harness expertise, since the Mexican authorities are of the opinion that a large part of the approximately 100,000 soldiers who have deserted the Mexican army over the seven-year period 2001–7, have joined the cartels. Los Zetas, a paramilitary force associated with the Gulf Cartel[25] (Mexico's largest drug cartel), is still actively recruiting personnel from the Mexican armed forces and from law enforcement.[26]

Box 4.1 Los Zetas

Los Zetas ("Zeta" is federal police/army radio abbreviation for "high-ranking officer") are former Mexican Army special forces personnel, who were trained in locating and apprehending drug cartel members. They now constitute a highly disciplined private army operating under the orders of the Gulf Cartel, one of several drug trafficking organizations in Mexico. The Gulf Cartel is "headquartered" in and around Reynosa on the Rio Grande across from southern Texas. It is estimated that Los Zetas is approximately 200 strong and headed by one Heriberto Lazcano. They are armed with military equipment and arms at the level of sophistication of the Mexican Army. They also operate modern wiretapping equipment and by corruption obtain the cellular telephone codes necessary for the intercept. They are known to have retained local gangs to execute contract killings. Los Zetas is obviously not the only drug enforcer gang in the world, far from it, nor the only private mercenary army in the service of organized crime. The group, however, has a series of characteristics worth highlighting: (i) the high level of professionalism; (ii) the direct hiring of elite federal police and military personnel; (iii) the occasional outsourcing of tasks to street gangs such as MS-13; (iv) intense use of corruption; and (v) the use of sophisticated telephone intercept material.

It should be noted that the U.S. Drug Enforcement Administration (DEA) operates a different definition of narco-terrorism, namely "an organized group that is complicit in the activities of drug trafficking in order to further, or fund, premeditated, politically motivated violence perpetrated against noncombatant targets with the intention to influence" (that is, influence a government or group of people).[27] This conceptual entry point shifts the emphasis; on the Makarenko scale, the Mylonaki definition concerns point 2 on the left-hand side, while the DEA definition, point 2 on the right-hand side.

It is not clear to what degree terrorists and organized criminals cooperate in other parts of the world, but so-called *pentiti* in Italy, former criminals who "regret"—as the term *pentito* stresses—and now assist the judicial authorities, have pointed to a series of meetings in Western Sicily between terrorist groups from the Middle East and Italian organized crime elements, in particular Francesco Messina Denaro, the Trapani (Sicily) Mafia "boss."[28] The veracity of such statements has not yet been confirmed, and a fair amount of skepticism should be exercised when evaluating allegedly repentant criminals' statements and their motives. The criminal operations of an organization that is normally seen as a pure terrorist organization, Hezbollah, were found to include intellectual property crime, cigarette smuggling, drug trafficking, and the African diamond trade.[29] Hezbollah, which was designated a Foreign Terrorist Organization by the U.S. Department of State in 1997,[30] reportedly "earned an estimated profit of $1.5 million in the United States between 1996 and 2000 by purchasing cigarettes in a low tax state for a lower price and selling them in a high tax state at a higher price."[31] Also, 14 of the 36 organizations on the U.S. State Department list have been linked with drug trafficking.[32]

As noted above, terrorists may use organized crime methodology and vice versa. Such use is not without its danger, however, to the concerned parties; organized criminals might attract unwarranted attention if they attack the governmental apparatus in a visible way ("high profile attention drawing actions tend to be anathema to the Mafioso"[33]), while terrorists may slowly lose sight of their ideological goals under the influence of the luxuries of a comfortable life based on easy gains.[34]

A refreshing view on terrorism is provided by the Indian scholar Kshitij Prabha, who emphasizes the point that "Current profiles of terrorist groups present a unique blend of rigidity in commitment to the cause and flexibility in operation that makes the task of countering terrorism difficult."[35] For the present discussion, the idea of "flexibility in operation" is particularly crucial as it underlines the attitude to the involvement or non-involvement in organized crime activities.

Intellectual property crime

Intellectual property crime, IPC, more commonly called *counterfeiting*, has been identified as a major source of income for terrorist organizations. The overall market value of counterfeit goods has been estimated by the WCO at $500 billion per year; approximately one half of this accrues from the sale of counterfeit goods in the United States. The investment to earnings ratio is approximately the same as the one that obtains for narcotic drugs, 1:10 (1 dollar invested, 10 dollars earned), and the penalties, if caught, are negligible compared with the illicit traffic in drugs.[36] The entry-level investment and knowledge requirements are— obviously depending on the sector—very limited. A counterfeit audio CD costs €0.20 to produce and only requires a very basic modern computer for the production, plus a label printer. Finally, this particular crime, IPC, does not cause the same opprobrium as other profitable crimes, which do not require particular skills or citizenship, such as drugs trafficking, pimping, and violent crime.

It is therefore small wonder that many terrorist organizations have chosen intellectual property crime as an easy and relatively risk-free means of funding. The first terrorist organization to have used counterfeiting for fundraising may very well have been the IRA, which already in the early 1980s sold counterfeit veterinary medicines before moving on to counterfeit CDs and DVDs. Since this organization also controls the markets throughout at least parts of Northern Ireland, it has no difficulty in placing the counterfeit goods for sale.

It is not of core interest to enumerate the terrorist groups that engage in these activities, from Kosovo to South America (via the Tri-Border Area).[37] It is, however, worth noting that as considerable efforts have been made to limit or eliminate the smuggling of brand cigarettes, the countries in the developed world, where tobacco products have been de-reified and instead monetized, are now ripe for a serious onslaught of counterfeit tobacco products, which will profit organized crime and terrorist organizations alike.

Financing of terrorism

The financing of terrorist activities, "combating terrorist financing" (CTF) was not studied in depth before the terrorist attacks perpetrated in the United States on 11 September 2001. The reason for this was, presumably, that most, but by no means all, terrorist organizations concentrated their activities in one country, where they also raised the—mostly very modest—funds needed; examples here are the Rote

Armee Fraktion (Germany), the Red Brigades (Italy), and Combatant Communist Cells (Belgium). In fact, when thinking about the financing of terrorism, it is useful to visualize three concentric circles, which indicate the quantitative differences between the functions exercised within the organization. This resultant image of terrorism is based on empirical evidence, is very approximate, and will certainly not earn the approval of a majority of scholars (see Figure 4.2).

The inner circle consists of persons who are willing and capable of killing. Since the terrorist organizations mentioned above operated in representative democracies, in non-insurgency situations, and without any general support from the population, the number of individuals in this circle, randomly designated as x, is very limited.[38]

The second concentric circle consists of people whose role within the organization is logistic. They are neither willing nor capable of killing; however, they are fully aware of and support the activities of the individuals in the inner circle, for whom they rent apartments, obtain motor vehicles, and provide the daily necessities. The number of individuals in this second circle is x^2.

Finally, individuals in the outer circle are donors, who can claim to give to a good cause and feign ignorance of the existence and activities of the individuals in the inner circle. Their role in the organization is limited to raising funds. Although overall supportive of the activities of the individuals in the inner circle, they have *deniable knowledge*. The number of individuals in this third circle is $x^{2*2} = x^4$.

It should be stressed that the use of the circles does not indicate that all or most persons in one circle know all or most of the other people in the same circle. Some of the individuals in the second circle know some of the individuals in the outer circle; likewise some of the persons in the second circle know some of those in the inner circle, but it is not

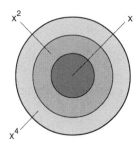

Figure 4.2 The concentric circles of terrorism
Source: Present author.

given that any one person in the second circle knows individuals in both the inner and outer circles. This proviso serves to allow for this model to be applicable also to terrorist cell structures. It should also be stressed that this imagined depiction is for illustrative purposes, only, since there definitely exists terrorism which does not fit the pattern, for example very small, independent terrorist cells; likewise, the multiplication factor of the power of two, when moving from the inner to the middle and from the middle to the outer circle is very approximate, but not necessarily wrong, since it was elaborated on an empirical basis in the European terrorism environment of the 1970s.

As pointed out above, not all "pre-9/11 terrorism" was confined to one territory; there were at least three major exceptions. First, the IRA, which—although it confined its terrorist operations to one country, the United Kingdom—established a substantial part of its fundraising in the northeastern United States, with the full, yet deniable, knowledge of the donors as well as of the government of the United States. Second, while the LTTE operationally was and is active in Sri Lanka, yet funding originates from the Tamil diaspora around the world. Third, various Middle East terrorist groups such as the PFLP.

For the present purposes, the Middle East terrorist groups are the most noticeable. They have committed terrorist attacks outside of a given territory, from Vienna, Austria, to Israel, but also their funding has had worldwide sources, in the form of donations as well as the proceeds of criminal activity. The terrorist organizations from the Middle East from the 1970s and 1980s can be taken to be precursors of today's Middle East terrorists in many ways, including their global outlook in target selection and funding sources. They differ, however, on two important points:

(i) the pre-9/11 Middle East terrorists did commit terrorist acts outside of the Middle East, but they traveled to do so; they did not rely on local sympathizers—or "franchises"—to engage in the actual terrorist acts as has become the case now; and

(ii) many, albeit not all, pre-9/11 Middle East terrorist groups were influenced by Marxism or Maoism, not religious ideology. Thus, in 1968, eight of the eleven (73 percent) identifiable terrorist organizations could be characterized as "left-wing, revolutionary Marxist-Leninist ideological organizations, the remaining three being ethnonationalist Palestinian groups."[39] By 1995, 26 of the 56 then known, active international terrorist groups were predominantly religious in nature and as of October 2005, 50 percent (21 of 42) of organizations classed as International Terrorist Organizations by the U.S. State Department, were religious in nature.[40]

This development is of interest as some scholars, of whom Siobhan O'Neil is one, opine that the Marxist-Leninist groups were less inclined to engage in terrorist funding by criminal activity since this, in some sense, would tarnish the image they had created or were creating for themselves. One can speculate that religiously inspired groups might take the view that although criminality such as theft and fraud is against the religious tenets to which they adhere, the pursuit of an ultimate, in their eyes highly laudable goal would invalidate such prohibitions. Indeed, the extremist movement Takfir wal-Hijra (Excommunication and Hegira) or, commonly Takfir, encourages theft and drug trafficking, on condition that one-fifth of the proceeds of the crime be destined for the Islamic cause.[41]

Two cases, displaying many similar traits albeit from almost opposite sides of the world (Los Angeles and Denmark) illustrate the funding mechanism referred to above. In a case investigated 2000–2 in Los Angeles, but the operations of which are believed still to be ongoing, U.S. customs intercepted an outgoing box, addressed to an individual in the Lebanon. The box, shipped from a textile company in the Los Angeles area, contained coats, in which, between the coat itself and the lining, had been inserted (sewed) $280,000. The textile business whence the box had been shipped was running at a loss, and it was suspected that the funds originated from drug trafficking. A search of the sender's premises disclosed a further $1.5 million; this individual was the brother of a Hizbollah operative who had recently been killed by the Israeli armed forces.[42]

The second example concerns terrorist funding by criminality by a 1970s–1980s Palestinian group, the PFLP. On 23 March 1983, in Lyngby, Denmark, a number of individuals committed an armed robbery against a money transport and secured DKr6 million ($655,638 at the then exchange rate of $1 = DKr 9.15). Three days later, two Palestinians were arrested at Charles de Gaulle Airport in Paris as they attempted to board Air France flight 142 for Damascus. In the course of the boarding security process, security operatives discovered a considerable amount of Danish currency concealed in the space between the outer tissue and the lining of the jackets the two men wore, and subsequent examination of their luggage disclosed further Danish currency, leading to a total of DKr6 million. They were relatively easily identified by the security services as the "head and treasurer for Western Europe" of the PFLP, Ghazi Massoud, and the "head" of the Federal Republic of Germany (FRG) arm of the PFLP, Mohammed Toman.

A Danish official attempted to act as interpreter and as negotiator in Paris for four parties at the same time, namely the Danish police, the

French police, the Danish intelligence services and the French intelligence services.[43] The French authorities, however, refused the Danish authorities access to the seized bills and refused to exchange these against fresh bills from the Central Bank of Denmark, most certainly for fear that fingerprints or body fluids on the seized money would establish a firm relationship between the funds seized, the two arrestees, and the crime committed three days earlier in Denmark. The money was seized and the two individuals expelled. The attitude of the Danish authorities was equally ambiguous.

As illustrated in Chapter 3 ("Operation Green Quest"), the events narrated above conform to the general pattern which I attempt to show, namely that terrorism to a large degree is funded by common criminality and that the "route of the funds" is from the developed world to the Middle East, and not necessarily the opposite. Second, the resolution of the Paris end of the case, if one can call it a resolution, showed unequivocally that the fear that governments exhibit when faced with international terrorism supersedes any treaty obligations. In the case at hand, it is clear that the French authorities wanted to expel the two individuals before a link between the robbery on 23 March 1983 in Denmark and the seizure of the money three days later in Paris could be proven. Had such proof been obtained, the Danish authorities would have had great difficulty in not requesting the extradition of the two individuals, and the French authorities would have had considerable difficulties in denying it, considering that both countries were and are members of the Council of Europe and that both are frequent signatories of (bombastic) declarations of the hard line that they—sometime in the future—will take against violent crime and terrorism. The French authorities' fear of having the two individuals in prison or of having to extradite them to what would have been a lengthy custodial sentence, quite clearly assisted the Danish authorities in not having to ask for an extradition, which they were afraid to do—for the same reason.

I argue that here, again, one is faced with deviant knowledge, since the decision-makers were in possession of the knowledge, which would have allowed the arrest and sentencing of two individuals responsible for the robbery (by profiting from it). The exercise of deviant knowledge by the French and perhaps—even presumably—also by the Danish authorities not only protected the two Palestinian terrorists, but also the group which had executed the crime in Denmark. Once the two individuals had been set free, the link between the money seized and the original crime, the armed robbery, was easily proven. However, the application of deviant knowledge—as one could have presumed—had as a result that not only could the two individuals continue their terrorist activities, but their contacts in Denmark could continue their terrorist fundraising criminal acts, too. The latter consisted in a small group of seven males, formed into a Maoist cell. After the events described above—as a result of which they were not identified—they continued their criminal fundraising means by committing at least three major armed robberies, in the course of one of which they shot and killed a police official.

I argue that there is no fundamental difference between lawyers, accountants, and other professionals who for short-term gain place themselves and their knowledge at the disposal of people who need to launder monetary funds, and those civil servants who deviate the use of their knowledge in order to circumvent laws, in particular international agreements, to assist the political powers who hold sway at that particular moment.

By way of a conclusion to this chapter on organized crime and terrorism, I would argue that the main problem is that there is no accepted definition of either term. For many years, the United Nations has attempted but failed to arrive at a definition of terrorism which would be acceptable to its membership. The efforts have failed, I would sustain, for two reasons. First, many countries, including many in the developed world, want to retain the capability of deciding, on a case-by-case basis, who is and who is not a terrorist or a terrorist financier; one thinks for example of the ambiguity of the position of the various U.S. governments over the last 30 years towards the Irish-American community in the United States as obvious financers of terrorism in Great Britain.[44] Second, many countries, mostly in the developing world, insist on having a definition of terrorism include what they refer to as "causes," typically poverty, despair, and the Palestine question. Although one can understand—and some may perhaps share—the (political) reasoning behind such demands, they are nevertheless not very helpful, as such "causes" would exclude, inter alia, the major endogenous terrorist movements that were active in Western Europe in the 1970s, which certainly were not "caused" by poverty, despair, or the Palestinian question. In the case of organized crime, the situation is not much better, since there is a large and growing number of definitions of organized crime.

Present scholarship concentrates on certain "overlaps" between the two species; I would argue that this is not the best approach to analyzing the problem. Instead, one presumably would need to examine the concepts of *intent* and *motivation*. The intent for specific acts committed by the two groups might overlap, their motivations do not; the terrorist's is purely political, the organized criminal's is purely financial. A third concept, which undoubtedly would need further serious treatment in this context, is that of *identity*. One would need to establish how "the world" sees each group, in other words which identity we establish for them, and how they see themselves, that is which identity they establish for themselves. One needs also to consider how both change, depending on which facet one is observing, which, again, is the result both of the point of view of the observer and the conscious or unconscious choice made by the observed of which side of his or her complex identity to expose to the observer.

The relationship between organized crime and terrorism, which this chapter has considered, is fully based on the issue of funding; the next chapter, Chapter 5, therefore pursues this subject by enquiring into the general area of economics and organized crime.

5 The economics of transnational organized crime

In 1958, George Vold introduced the concept of "the economic determinist approach," namely "the proposition that economic life is fundamental and therefore the determining influence upon which all social and cultural arrangements are made."[1] The idea here is that the "economic life" has a determining influence on crime in general and transnational organized crime in particular.

Since the 1960s, the relationship between crime and economics has been the subject of scholarly debate. For example, the economist Loretta Napoleoni claims that one of the most far-reaching and damaging effects of the deregulation of markets, in particular the financial markets, has been, first, the emergence of the "new economy of terror," the international economic system run primarily by armed organizations to self-finance the armed struggle and, second, "the merging of the new economics of terror with the international illegal and criminal economy."[2]

Organized crime and globalization

Much contemporary scholarly debate about organized crime and economics refers to globalization as an explanatory component. Panić, however, notes with regard to globalization that: "There is little agreement about the meaning of the term, even less agreement about the processes that bring globalization about, and no agreement at all about its effects."[3] Some scholars agree with Robin Thomas Naylor and do not believe that there has been an economic globalization measured as international trade (global imports plus global exports) versus world gross domestic product (GDP).[4] Furthermore, they doubt that contemporary technological developments have had a major influence on illegality compared, say, with the development of the steam engine and the telegraph.

It is important to emphasize that the concepts touched upon above are not synonyms for another hotly disputed term, the gross criminal product (GCP), but that they are much wider. In fact, GCP may constitute only one-third of the funds of non-declared origin, with which the present work is concerned.[5] It is presumably not possible, at our present state of knowledge, to evaluate the so-called GCP in any meaningful manner. The chapter will, nevertheless, approach this problem by examining, as a starting point, the claims made by Napoleoni.

Transnational crime as part of globalization has expanded its international traffic of various kinds, in arms, humans, drugs, etc. Such traffics necessitate payment settlement in order to be completed and, therefore, a means of payment, which necessarily must be easy to transport, non-traceable, highly liquid and readily acceptable almost globally. The U.S. currency has, traditionally, played this role. It is self-evident that it is not possible to measure the use of U.S. currency for the settlement of international criminal traffics. Nevertheless, as a proxy, albeit admittedly not a very precise one, though viable for the present purpose, the chapter will attempt to examine the important question of *expatriate U.S. currency*, that is to say U.S. currency in the form of dollar notes circulating in the world outside the United States.

International crime represents both a cultural and a political exemplification of the internal logic of globalization; if, as the present writer, one perceives international organized crime as a reflection of society in a broad sense, including international society, then there is nothing particularly strange in this phenomenon, which obtains in complete parallel with globalization, namely that organized crime at one and the same time extends its reach internationally, and concurrently strengthens its local grip, thus exemplifying the neologism, *glocal*.

Two terms are used in this field and can give rise to confusion. One is the *political economy of crime*, which refers to the possible influence of economic factors such as poverty and inequality on crime levels.[6] In the present context, however, the term of interest is the *economics of crime*, which, on the empirical level, typically refers to the question of the profits that organized crime may generate and, on the theoretical level, to the much more substantive question of organized crime as an economic actor. Among scholars there is an ongoing, rather heated debate between those, like Claudio Besozzi,[7] who think that the profits of crime are over-estimated and those who take a more alarmist view of the role of "criminal" profits in the world economy, for instance Guilhem Fabre.[8]

A second debate has as its main opponents those who—apart from their concern about the profits of crime—are worried about the reach of crime and therefore study crime as a global phenomenon. For example, on the one hand consider Jean Ziegler[9] and Louise Shelley,[10] and, on the other, a minority of scholars who are very critical of the issue of organized crime in general and transnational organized crime in particular. The latter argue that the phenomenon is being exaggerated by the law enforcement community with a view to obtain increased budget allocations, and by the political class as a means of gaining democratic consensus for societal control mechanisms which otherwise would not have been acceptable. They point to two main areas, which they see as representative: the "militarization" of interior security and the growing influence of international law on public national policy. These scholars are perhaps best represented by David Nelken[11] and Maria Luisa Cesoni.[12] When evaluating these arguments, however, one needs to keep in mind Anthony Giddens' general definition of "modernization" as "a capitalist system of commodity production, industrialism, developed state surveillance techniques, and militarized order."[13] One might therefore ask if control mechanisms, militarization, and so forth, are organic reactions to the complexities of modern and post-modern society rather than conscious designs on the part of government officials or the political class. As regards the more crucial problem and consequent analysis of the function of organized crime as an economic actor[14] or as organized crime in the international economy, Mark Findlay quite rightly observes—with regard to the management of global economic interdependence—that:

> Just as international treaties are becoming identified with such management initiatives, and crime is identified amongst the problems to be "managed," so too the internationalization of crime control is being promoted as a reaction to the assumed expansion of crime in a global economic context [...] The economies of crime and crime control are now squarely within global political discourse.[15]

The scope of the problem

Napoleoni claims that the "new economy of terror" (a concept developed in her 2003 book, *Modern Jihad*) has merged with the international illegal and criminal economy. The resultant yearly flows of funds, which she calculates at 1.5 trillion dollars, consist in three parts, each of $500 billion: (i) *capital flight*, money, which "moves illegally from country to country, undetected and unreported";[16] (ii) the *gross criminal product*, money generated primarily by criminal organizations;[17]

and (iii) the *new economy of terror*, money produced by terrorist organizations, of which approximately one-third is from legitimate businesses and the rest from criminal activities, primarily the drug trade and smuggling.[18] In summary form, the three categories are: illegal, criminal, and terror funds, the latter consisting partly in funds of legitimate origin. The resultant 1.5 trillion dollars flows into the European and North American economies every year and constitutes a vital element in the cash flow of these economies.

Raymond W. Baker paints an alarmist image of the noxiousness of money laundering for the United States as well as for the international economy in his 2005 book as well as in his 1999 testimony to the U.S. Senate. His main concern is that so-called capital flight is used as a cover for money laundering, "thereby weakening our ability to prevail in facing some of the most perilous threats to our society." I contest Baker's view on three counts: first, it is not money laundering but the underlying predicate crimes that constitute a potential threat to society; second, an unstated premise for Baker's view is that an effective anti-money laundering regime would contribute to a decline in predicate crime; it will not and Baker's non-stated premise is the more surprising as he, himself, has arrived at the conclusion—correct in my view—that "Anti-money laundering efforts are a failure." One might add that the failure is very costly. Finally, one might raise the question whether so-called laundered funds, once injected into the international financial markets, do not, after all, constitute a vast benefit. The U.S. RICO provisions provide the beginning of an answer to this intricate question and will be treated separately.[19]

Surprisingly—and excitingly—Napoleoni makes the claim that not only are the above flows known or to a certain degree calculable, but so is their growth. She points out that there is a clear *interdependency between the growth of the terror, criminal and illegal economy, and the growth of the U.S. money supply.*[20] This is an exciting venue for investigation, for which see below.

The U.S. RICO provisions

One of the major preoccupations of the American legislator in producing the 1970 RICO Act[21] was not so much a concern that criminals succeed in obtaining and concealing their ill-gotten gains, rather it was the use to which such funds are put. 18 USC §1962(a) addresses this concern, since the legislator attempts to prevent organized crime from engaging in interstate or foreign commerce or from taking a controlling interest in a securities-issuing corporation. Elsewhere in this work,

I have asked the question whether funds obtained from criminal activity and injected into the legitimate economy constitute an activity which is pernicious or beneficial to the economy. The U.S. legislator as mirrored in the above legislation would appear to provide a beginning of an answer, namely that such funds are harmful to the economy either if they are used to constitute a commercial entity, or if their use entails the control by the criminal actor or his or her family or accomplices of a corporation. It is obviously not clear from this piece of legislation whether or not one can conclude, *e contrario*, that such funds, if placed in a non-controlling position, contribute positively to the economy, although one might be permitted to think so, since they help render the financial markets more liquid. The point, however, that the U.S. legislator seems to make is that funds originating from organized crime activities, if used to create commercial entities trading in interstate or foreign markets or to take control over securities-issuing corporations, are harmful to the economy—precisely because such companies, if necessary, will have access to almost unlimited funds and therefore will not be subject to the vagaries of the market, to which other companies need to submit. The capitalist system, the legislator seems to say, only functions in an environment of full equality on a level playing field.

The money supply

The U.S. Federal Reserve System issues new currency—M0 and M1 expand—in a way for which there has been no purely domestic explanation since the 1980s; only the exportation of such currency and its circulation abroad would be a satisfactory hypothesis. For the year 2000, as much as two-thirds of the currency component of M1, $500 billion excluding vault cash, was reportedly held abroad. It is probably the case that so much U.S. currency is held abroad because it is highly liquid, universally accepted, and untraceable.

Since this study excludes vault cash, bank holdings are ipso facto excluded and U.S. currency held outside of the United States can, from the standpoint of empirical logic, only take one of two forms; it is either circulating or it is being hoarded.

In the period of liberalization of the financial markets and of a considerable reduction in commerce restrictions, it is perhaps not surprising that also the amount of illegal traffic would appear to have increased, drugs, humans, arms, etc. It is reasonable to presume that the U.S. dollar—and in particular $100s—is the preferred means for settling such deals. Therefore, if illegal trafficking expands in a manner so significant that it would influence currency demand, then one would expect to see an expansion in U.S. money supply, too. Also, if in the period after the Second World War, in which the use of the U.S. dollars has been internationalized, the world traverses a period characterized by many large or relatively large civil wars, then one would expect the U.S. money supply to expand since at least one side in such intra-national conflicts would have to buy weapons, explosives, ammunition, and other supplies on the black market and, one may suppose, settle such purchases with hard currency.

There are many ways of evaluating the amount of U.S. expatriate currency and most of these are treated by Richard Porter and Ruth Judson,[22] and Brian Doyle.[23] There are likewise many explanations of this phenomenon; for example Theodore Allison and Rosanna Pianalto[24] believe that the liberalization and "democratization" of economic systems around the world have led to the creation of inflation and inadequate financial sectors. The latter have then induced the population in such countries to use the U.S. dollar both as a means of exchange at the business level and as a store of wealth at the household level.

In the period after the Second World War, household settlement methods were introduced in the developed world, which have consistently diminished the need for using cash: checks, direct debit arrangements, and, in particular, credit and debit cards.[25] One would expect the amount of currency outstanding to grow at approximately the growth rate of consumption or, rather, a little less, since the growth in consumption—and therefore the growth in payment settlements—is offset by the gradual shift in payment settlement patterns away from cash and toward non-cash settlement; in particular, credit and debit card payments have increased.[26] Furthermore, since household debt in the United States and in the United Kingdom has gone up as a percentage of household income at least from 1987, that fact alone—and even more so if combined with an increase in the use of non-cash payment methods—*must* mean that currency in circulation in the United States and United Kingdom has decreased substantially, since a larger and larger part of disposable income is absorbed by debt repayment, which does not involve the use of cash.[27] In this context, Figure 5.1 is very persuasive. It shows the ratio between $M1^c$ (the currency component of M1) and M2 for the period 1960 to 1995. As one would expect, the ratio sharply decreases, as funds are moved from non-interest bearing accounts in M1 to interest-bearing instruments in M2 and as the use of currency in the United States diminishes. From the mid-1980s, however, this trend is sharply reversed; again, the explanation can only be external demand for U.S. currency.

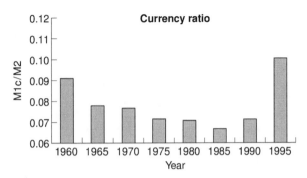

Figure 5.1 M1^c/M2, 1960–95. Quinquennial geometric means
Source: Underlying dataset from weekly Federal Reserve Statistical Releases;
calculations by present author.

The U.S. Federal Reserve System perceives U.S. dollar notes uniquely in terms of a commodity, which it provides to whomever is willing to buy.[28] Also, expatriate currency, *in casu* U.S. dollars, provides the issuing country, the United States, with an appreciable income through seigniorage.[29] According to the U.S. Department of the Treasury, in 2005 seigniorage totaled $29 billion, of which $21 billion in earnings, about 1 percent of federal receipts, was remitted to the Treasury.[30] In the same report, the Treasury estimates that nearly 60 percent of all banknotes in circulation, or about $450 billion of the $760 billion in circulation as of December 2005, were held abroad.[31]

Measuring expatriate currency

There are few direct data sources available on currency circulating outside of the issuing country. For example, for the United States there are two such sources, the U.S. Customs Service Reports of International Transportation of Currency and Other Monetary Instruments (CMIR)[32] and the reporting submitted to the Federal Reserve Bank of New York by commercial banks exporting funds. Of these, however, the former is not reliable, because of under- and possible double reports, and the latter is confidential and thus not available to researchers. Therefore, in order to evaluate the magnitude of such funds, one needs to use indirect procedures, which are not absolutely precise; nevertheless, since the results of several of the more common of the indirect methodologies converge, their overall robustness appears validated.

For the United States, the Federal Reserve Banks are responsible for the issue of U.S. dollar notes in all denominations (the issuance of coinage is under the tutelage of the U.S. Treasury Department) and also for receiving excess funds held by the more than 3,000 member banks. $20 bills are in more common use than $100s in the United States, but $100s make up 60 percent of the dollar value of all outstanding U.S. currency.[33] The Federal Reserve System also receives and destroys notes that are soiled, torn, or otherwise no longer useable; the amounts involved, however, are so small that they can be disregarded in the present context.

Federal Reserve notes (U.S. dollar notes) are exported by commercial banks. Unfortunately, although the commercial banks do report to the Federal Reserve System the amounts of notes exported, such data are considered proprietary information belonging to the banks in question and the Federal Reserve System cannot make the information available. Federal Reserve System statistics, however, show that, consistently, the New York City Federal Reserve Cash Office (FRCO) issues nearly all $100s; for example, it issued 83 percent of all $100s in the period from 1974 to 1995, inclusive.

A further restriction in the data collection and in research in the present context, and in the evaluation of expatriate currency in what some authors have called the "shadow economy," is that Federal Reserve researchers assume that all or the vast majority of U.S. dollar notes being exported are exported by commercial banks with the exception of small amounts that are imported and exported by traveling business persons or by tourists. That this is an obvious weakness is made clear both from anecdotal evidence of the use of so-called "body-wraps"[34] and by well known examples, the best known of which is the "Crazy Eddie" case, in which at least $7 million was taken out of the United States taped to the bodies of couriers.

Methods for evaluating currency held overseas

Several methods have been established to attempt to evaluate the scope of the flux of U.S. dollar bills out of the United States or, to put it differently, to estimate the scope of the fluxes of U.S. dollar bills outside of the United States, which I here summarize. The shipments methodology is the one adopted by the Federal Reserve System, the theoretical underpinnings of which are a further elaboration of the work, inter alia, of Edgar Feige. It rests on three presuppositions: (i) most foreign-held U.S. currency is in the form of $100s; (ii) all or most exports of $100s occur at one FRCO;[35] as most of the currency-exporting banks referred to above are located in New York City, it is obvious that the FRCO in New York City plays a predominant role; and (iii) no or little part of the flow of $100s through the cash offices mentioned under (ii) reflects changes in domestic (U.S.) demand for $100s.[36] Receipts and emissions of $10s from all 37 FRCOs follow relatively stable mean and seasonable patterns, as do $1s and $5s. Already $20s, however, "display relatively less constant mean and seasonal patterns."[37] For $100s, the question is very different. Before the 1980s, the FRCO in New York City had an issuance pattern of $100s which was not significantly different from the FRCOs in the rest of the United States. In other words, it is safe to draw the conclusion that the intensive use of the U.S. dollar outside of the United States commenced in the 1980s.

In an authoritative study by the U.S. Treasury Department, the authors, formed as a tripartite working group called the International Currency Awareness Program (ICAP) from the U.S. Treasury, the Federal Reserve System, and the U.S. Secret Service, emphasize that "Residents of many countries outside the United States use U.S. banknotes as a store of value and as a medium of exchange" and that U.S. dollars are often found in countries with volatile political and economic conditions.[38] It is not immediately clear, however, that the world had more volatile political and economic conditions after, say, the mid-1980s than before. I would argue that what did happen in the mid-1980s was an important expansion of illegal trafficking, in particular in drugs and arms, which required settlement in a portable, divisible, liquid currency, the U.S. dollar. Second, the argument that "residents of many countries outside the United States use U.S. banknotes as ... a means of exchange" is—to put it politely—dubious. Such usage cannot explain why the preferred overseas "means of exchange" should be the $100s, if, that is, such use was common day-to-day "means of exchange," which would necessitate banknotes of all denominations in order to be executed smoothly.

In their 1996 paper, Porter and Judson apply ten different methods to assess the amount of U.S. currency in circulation outside of the United States and use the median of the results thus obtained to estimate expatriate U.S. currency.[39] The two economists arrive at results that are not significantly different from those obtained by Richard Anderson and Robert Rasche in their 2000 study:[40]

- $200–250 billion of U.S. currency was abroad at the end of 1995, which constituted 53.3–66.7 percent of the then outstanding base of approximately $375 billion in circulation outside of banks (the currency component of M1).
- The proportion of U.S. currency outside of the U.S.—expatriate U.S. currency—of all issued U.S. currency, had been steadily rising.

- Growth in foreign demand for U.S. currency and in particular for U.S. $100s was far stronger than growth in U.S. demand.
- Over the 1990s, overseas stock of U.S. currency grew at a rate of approximately three times the growth of the domestic stock.

Evaluation of the results

From the mid-1980s, substantial amounts of U.S. currency have been shipped overseas through the banking system. In the period 1988–91, the bulk was sent to the South and Latin America, in particular to Argentina, but from 1991 the major part has been shipped to Europe. In the two years 1994 and 1995, Russia alone received in excess of $20 billion each year.[41] For the whole period, 1988–95 inclusive, the split is indicated in Figure 5.2.

Figure 5.3 conclusively depicts the concurrent decrease in growth in domestically held currency and the concurrent—remarkable—increase in the growth in overseas-held U.S. currency.

A last, important issue remains, however, namely that of *currency velocity*. The American economist Edgar Feige has undertaken a study in which he compared wear and tear of notes returned from abroad with notes returned from the United States as a proxy use. He found no difference. Therefore,

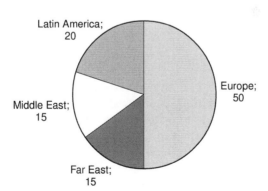

US currency shipment (%)

Latin America; 20
Europe; 50
Middle East; 15
Far East; 15

Figure 5.2 Shipments of U.S. currency by destination (%), 1988–95.
Source: Richard D. Porter and Ruth A. Judson, "The location of U.S. currency: How much is abroad?" *Federal Reserve Bulletin* (October 1996), 886.

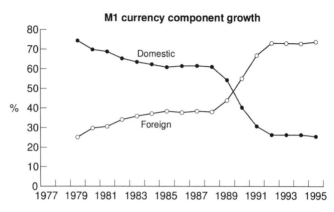

Figure 5.3 M1 currency component growth. Triennial moving geometric means
Source: Elaborated from dataset in Richard D. Porter and Ruth A. Judson,
"The location of U.S. currency. How much is abroad?" *Federal Reserve Bulletin*
(October 1996): 896.

> the velocity of domestically held currency is on average not differ-
> ent from the velocity of foreign held currency, which means that
> foreigners' U.S. currency holding would generate a flow of annual
> cash payments approaching the size of the GDP of the U.S.

His conclusion makes a very suitable end to this subsection: "The
world economy appears to subsume a U.S.-sized unrecorded economy
that employs U.S. currency as its medium of exchange."[42]
   As an example of the exportation of illegally obtained cash, the next
section consists of a case study of the Crazy Eddie electronic goods chain.

Case study: Crazy Eddie

Crazy Eddie was a chain of stores in New York selling electronics, and
was started in 1971 by Eddie Antar and his father, Sam M. Antar. The
chain's exuberant advertising on local television and radio was well
known to anybody who visited the states of New York or New Jersey
while the company was still active. Yearly sales at the peak of the
company's life were in excess of $300 million. Co-founder Eddie Antar
cashed in millions of dollars worth of stock and resigned from the
company in December 1986. In February 1987, the U.S. Attorney's
Office for the District of New Jersey commenced a federal grand jury
investigation into the financial activities of Crazy Eddie, and in September 1987 the Securities and Exchange Commission (SEC) initiated

an investigation into alleged violations of federal securities laws by certain company officers and employees. Eddie Antar became the focus of SEC and federal investigations, and he was eventually charged with a series of crimes.

He fled to Israel in February 1990, but was returned to the United States in January 1993 to stand trial. His 1993 conviction on fraud charges was overturned, but he eventually pleaded guilty in 1996 and in 1997 was sentenced to eight years in prison and received fines of $150 million.

Almost from the beginning, Crazy Eddie's management was engaged in various forms of fraud. The Antars paid employees off the books, and regularly skimmed thousands of dollars (in cash) earned at the stores. For every $5 Crazy Eddie reported as income, $1 was taken off the books by the Antars. In 1979, the Antars began depositing much of this money in overseas bank accounts. The Antar family skimmed an estimated $3–4 million per year at the height of their fraud. In one offshore bank account, the family deposited more than $6 million between 1980 and 1983. After a hostile take-over in 1987, the new owners instituted a preliminary audit. The auditors estimated that Crazy Eddie's inventory was short by $40–50 million, but the final figure was twice as much, $80 million.[43]

Errors and omissions

The definitional properties of the balance of payments ensure that when some countries have pluses in their balance of payments, others have corresponding minuses. In actual calculations, there have always been minor discrepancies; things have not quite added up to zero. But the minor differences could be disregarded as "errors and omissions." From the late 1970s, however, computations of the world balance of payments revealed systematic and growing discrepancies. One such calculation showed that by the early 1980s the world was running an annual balance-of-payments deficit with itself in the vicinity of $100 billion.[44] In other words, it was running a balance of payments deficit with the Moon equal to about 10 percent of the total value of world market trade.

The IMF, using an unpublished U.S. Federal Reserve Board study, proposes four possible causes for the discrepancy: (i) transportation delays, (ii) asymmetric valuation, (iii) data quality, and (iv) under-reporting of investment income.[45] Of interest in the present context is point (ii), *asymmetric valuation*, which the IMF explains by a difference in import and export pricing due to the use of differing foreign exchange rates or the registration in one country of the export at full price, but in the other the registration of the import at a subsidized price. I would suggest that there are more likely explanations, namely a voluntary under-reporting of an export or over-reporting of an import in order to move funds in and out of jurisdictions with currency restraints, or to effectuate money laundering. Point (iv), *under-reporting of investment income,* is undoubtedly linked to investment income in offshore financial centers.

At the heart of all the arguments about mafias and organized crime lies the issue of denied demand which is highly criminogenic; financial services are no exception to this general rule. Until this point, this book has considered the character and manifestations of transnational organized crime. States have attempted to counter transnational criminal acts, and the next chapter will examine these attempts.

6 Initiatives against transnational crime

The various counter-measures which so far have been fielded against transnational organized crime were developed at both national and international level; they consist in institutions (including procedures) and legislation. After an introduction, which considers the processes of international crime control, the chapter is subdivided into two parts; the first part considers some of institutions involved in the attempt to counter transnational crime—the verb "counter" is chosen with some care, since we shall never be able to "interdict" such crime. In fact, as Durkheim observed, "The more the group is spread out, although densely concentrated, the more the collective attention, dissipated over a wide area, becomes incapable of following the movements of each individual [...]. The surveillance is less careful, because there are too many people and things to watch."[1] International institutions which play a role in the creation and enforcement of counter-measures include the United Nations system, Interpol, and a number of regional organizations, in particular Europol. Their history and present-day functioning will be examined. The second part of the chapter surveys relevant legislation, in particular the criminalization of money laundering. As an example of anti-money laundering efforts there is a review of the situation in Thailand.

The chapter on the one hand realizes and salutes the creation and development of international law enforcement cooperation, from informal initiatives in the nineteenth century to a somewhat more developed system today; it does, however, concurrently question the efficiency of some of the measures proposed, their cost, and their severe impact on privacy rights.

Historical remarks

These introductory remarks will first, very briefly, consider the historical development of international law enforcement, before a consideration of the amazing developments over the last quarter of a century.

International law enforcement cooperation—cooperation between professional, specialized law enforcement agencies—commenced in the latter half of the nineteenth century. Previously, enforcement of two crimes which today constitute international crimes in and by themselves, piracy and trafficking in slaves, had been undertaken by military forces, in particular by the Royal Navy of Great Britain as regards trafficking in slaves.

The beginning of professional law enforcement in modern times can be dated to 1749 and the creation in London, England, of the Bow Street Runners, so called from their "headquarters" situated in the offices of Henry Fielding, justice of the peace and novelist, in Bow Street. This modest beginning was followed up with the creation of La Sureté in Paris in 1812 by Vidocq, and the Metropolitan Police in London by Robert Peel in 1829. The world's first specialized corps of detectives was created within the Metropolitan Police in 1842.

International law enforcement cooperation, on the other hand, was spurred on, initially, by the desire to keep itinerant political agitators under surveillance, in particular after the year 1848, which was a turbulent one for most of Europe. Initially, international law enforcement was based more on personal acquaintance among a number of dynamic police officials than on a formalized procedural approach. A number of assassinations of heads of state later in the century (Tsar Alexander II in 1881 and French president Sidi Carnot in 1894) by anarchists further intensified the need for cooperation, but it was the murder of the popular "Sissi" (Elizabeth, Empress of Austria) in September 1898 in Geneva, Switzerland, by a young Italian anarchist that led to an international conference that same year in Rome, at which 54 delegates from 21 countries agreed to the so-called "Belgian" or "attentat" clause, whereby attacks on heads of state or their families were deemed extraditable offenses.[2]

Concurrent with the anarchist scare—not dissimilar to the fear of terrorism that periodically from the 1960s to the beginning of the twenty-first century has seized at least the Occident—another international crime threatened the very core of the nation-states: that of currency counterfeiting, in particular where the counterfeiter operated in one country and introduced the product of his or her handiwork in another. An 1861 case in the British High Court of Chancery, *The Emperor of Austria v. Day and Kossuth*, became a landmark case.[3] Kussoth had produced counterfeit currency in England, but for distribution and use in Hungary, and claimed that British courts did not have jurisdiction. The court decided otherwise. Currency counterfeiting was undertaken by ordinary criminals with a lucrative scope, but also by political agitators who wished to undermine the economy of the target country by introducing vast amounts of counterfeit currency—thus creating both inflation and lack of confidence in the currency. Many European countries therefore set up central offices dealing with currency counterfeiting and tasked with maintaining contacts with counterpart offices in other countries; a fair number of these offices developed into Interpol National Central Bureaux.

The recent period

In recent decades, the agitations of transnational organized crime have attracted the attention not only of economists (see Chapter 5), but also—and increasingly—of diplomats and international relations scholars, who have perceived organized crime as a threat to international security and stability; transnational organized crime has thus become a considerable concern for national and international decision makers. Scholars and practitioners have increasingly pointed to the connection between transnational organized crime and state fragility, armed conflict and terrorism, and have highlighted the complex and problematic relationships between trafficking in arms, human beings and drugs, and corruption and state failure.[4]

In consequence, a number of measures to counter the activities of transnational crime have been introduced as part of global governance, consisting in particular of a series of so-called international prohibition schemes. Such schemes are by no means of recent vintage; in fact, the first international prohibition scheme was the anti-piracy measures, which, although only codified in 1856, had already operated effectively for some time. Recently, however, and in particular after the end of the Second World War, a number of such regimes have been introduced, some of which have been relatively effective, others less.

The salient point, however, has been and remains international law enforcement cooperation, without which international prohibition schemes would have little value—other than as moral pointers.

Andreas and Nadelmann point to the significant fact that international law enforcement commenced around the turn of the twentieth century springing from a fear of terrorism (bombings and assassinations of politicians) and that the same fear—now elevated to one of "catastrophic criminality"—in the post-9/11 world has, again, led to a convergence of law enforcement and national security forces at national level and to an increased level of cooperation at international level.[5] Most unbiased observers would presumably welcome this development, which, however, also conceals a number of disquieting elements. First, the union of law enforcement and national security almost always constitutes an unholy marriage, the result of which is exemplified by McCarthyism in the United States, not to mention the even more nefarious agitations in Europe of this infelicitous couple in the years leading up to the Second World War. The overemphasis on national security to the detriment of law enforcement can easily lead to a frantic search for national security threats, where none are readily available; unfortunately this search seems inexorably to lead to the identification of enemies within, in the form of a particular ethnicity or creed or members of a particular political persuasion. Second, the intensification of international law enforcement cooperation beginning approximately in the 1970s was spurred on by the developments in narcotics law enforcement and facilitated by globalization. The development of international narcotics law enforcement was very much a U.S. initiative and as "far as international law enforcement cooperation is concerned, 'globalization' is a synonym for 'Americanization,'"— achieved partly by coercion and partly by cooptation.[6] As Nadelmann notes, "there is, clearly, no one explanation for the internationalization of US criminal law enforcement,"[7] and national law enforcement organizations may, quite naturally, be reticent to share sensitive criminal intelligence with analysts, who, although of undoubted integrity and competence, represent just one country's interests. In consequence, the presently undisputed international law enforcement hegemony exercised by the United States will, in the long term, have to yield to more collegiate, multilateral arrangements. Both Interpol and UNODC can play a significant role here, on the global level, as both at times have demonstrated that they can offer highly credible analyses precisely because of their independence from national interests and their access to a wider range of data sources.

The most surprising element, however, in the development of international law enforcement cooperation has been its almost total concentration on the financial aspect under the general slogan of "taking the proceeds away from the criminals." The creation of the international cooperative pattern fully reflects this choice. As pointed out elsewhere in this book, a number of scholars, and indeed the present author, contend that this approach is conceptually ill-founded, unacceptably intrusive, and, ultimately, inefficient—apart from displacing the criminal justice discourse from an area of mostly common opprobrium (the predicate crimes) to regulatory offences. As regards the financing of terrorism, the money laundering approach seems particularly unsuited and, based on past experience, almost certain to fail, as Barry Rider points out: "(T)he success that law enforcement agencies have had around the world in 'taking the profit out of crime' is very limited and does not commend itself as a particularly efficient strategy in the fight against terrorists."[8]

Institutions

It should be recorded that in the preceding centuries, Britain's Royal Navy had played a significant role in international law enforcement in two crucial areas, anti-piracy and anti-slave trafficking. As the Navy's role petered out a vacuum was left, which only slowly was filled by national law enforcement agencies.

Interpol

In the period from 1899 to 1914, a series of police conferences throughout the world set the stage for more intensified cooperation. Some of these dealt with the suppression of the white slave trade, then something of an obsession, the response to which was incommensurate with the actual problem. A 1902 meeting in Paris led to the establishment in the 16 participating countries of specialized white slavery offices, which cooperated with each other across borders. It was, however, the 1914 international police meeting in Monte Carlo, which—almost—led to the creation of formalized international criminal police cooperation. Unfortunately, the meeting took place just before World War I, which put the project on hold. In 1923, the head of Vienna's police, Johann Schober, organized a meeting in Vienna, which led to the establishment in Vienna of the International Criminal Police Commission (ICPC). Interpol (the organization's telegraphic address) was born and it retained the ICPC name until 1956, when it moved to France and was renamed the International Criminal Police Organization—Interpol (ICPO).

The purpose of the organization is to facilitate cooperation between the 186 member countries' criminal police departments, which it does by placing a sophisticated communications system at the disposal of member countries, as well as information from the organization's extensive criminal records and fingerprint dataset at the organization's General Secretariat in Lyons, France. ICPO is managed in a rather classical way by a supreme organ, the General Assembly, which has created an Executive Committee, acting as the decision making entity between General Assembly meetings. The General Secretariat carries out the day-to-day work, in particular in cooperation with the National Central Bureaux (NCBs), of which there is one in each member country.

Interpol possesses many qualities that are and, in the present author's opinion, will remain unique. One of these is that the Secretariat can at short notice create an ad hoc working group on a specific subject, consisting of officers from the Secretariat as well as of officers and expertise borrowed from member countries via the appropriate NCBs. Such working groups can include some of the best expertise available in the world and stand out by being, and by being seen to be, independent.

On the negative side remains the less than ideal relationship the organization has had with the United States since the days when J. Edgar Hoover was the director of the Federal Bureau of Investigation. Also, most of the professional law enforcement staff of the General Secretariat in Lyons are police officials seconded from their respective countries; for various reasons, Interpol has not always been able to attract the most qualified and most dynamic officials. Finally, Interpol has always been grossly underfunded; for 2006, for example, the statutory contributions paid by the 186 member countries amounted to €37 million.

Interpol is increasingly seen as a valid professional partner at the highest possible levels, in particular because of the leadership of its relatively new Secretary-General, Ronald K. Noble. Thus, in 2004 in relation to the passing of the United Nations Security Council resolution on access to weapons of mass destruction by non-state actors,[9] U.S. President George W. Bush encouraged Proliferation Security Initiative (PSI) participants and other willing participants to "use the Interpol and all other means to bring to justice those who traffic in deadly weapons." Also, the UN Security Council has requested the Secretary-General of the United Nations to increase cooperation between the United Nations and Interpol, and has urged the UN membership to use the international police organization's resources in order better to implement the Security Council's decisions (on freezing of assets and travel bans). Indeed, to render cooperation between the two organizations more effective, in November 2004 Interpol appointed a very high-ranking police official (a former president of the German Federal Criminal Police, BKA) as the first Special Representative of Interpol to the United Nations, and thus created an Interpol office at the UN headquarters in New York.

Europol (EU)

The establishment of Europol was agreed in the Maastricht Treaty on European Union in 1992; its headquarters, the Directorate, is in The Hague, the Netherlands. From only being involved in the fight against drugs, the organization has developed its remit and now deals with crime on a thematic basis according to a listing annexed to the Europol Convention, which came into force in 1998. The mission statement of Europol declares that "Europol is the European Union law enforcement organisation that handles criminal intelligence. Its aim is to improve the effectiveness and cooperation between the competent authorities of the Member States in preventing and combating serious international organised crime and terrorism." The most important crimes with which Europol deals, according to its mandate, are illicit drug trafficking; terrorism; counterfeiting of the euro and other means of payment; trafficking in human beings (including child pornography); and money laundering.

Europol works along the lines of Interpol, at least to a certain degree, and a number of liaison officers are based at the Europol Directorate, where they facilitate the exchange of information, in accordance with national law. The organization issues a number of strategic reports; particularly important in the present context is the yearly Organised Crime Threat Assessment. The organization is better financed than Interpol; the Directorate's budget is almost double that of Interpol's General Secretariat.

From a governance point of view, the organization reports to the Council of Ministers for Justice and Home Affairs, which also appoints Europol's Director and Deputy Directors. It cooperates with a number of "third parties" (countries and organizations) in accordance with a series of cooperation agreements.

Closely linked with the evolution of Europol is that of two other institutions, Eurojust and the Council of Europe. Eurojust was created in 2002 as a complement to Europol, as an organization which would promote the cooperation in the European Union of the prosecutorial authorities by the "co-ordination of investigations and prosecutions between competent authorities in the Member States," in particular "by facilitating the execution of international mutual legal assistance and the implementation of extradition requests."[10]

The Council of Europe, on the other hand, was created in 1949; it thus predates the establishment of the European Communities and it has a larger membership of 47 states at the time of writing. It is headquartered in Strasbourg, France, where each member country has a permanent representative, most of ambassadorial level. The Council of Europe "seeks to develop throughout Europe common and democratic principles based on the European Convention on Human Rights and other reference texts on the protection of individuals."[11] Among the concerns of the organization, several are of core importance in the present context, in particular terrorism, trafficking in human beings, organized crime and corruption, cyber-crime, and violence against children.

The European Council has played, and continues to play, a core role in Europe in the fight against organized crime, and in 1997 adopted an Action Plan to combat organized crime, which was prepared by a high-level group of experts from the member states. Several of the recommendations of this Action Plan aim at improving the standards of cooperation between judicial authorities in criminal matters, which was one of the main arguments for the creation of Eurojust (see above).

United Nations

The United Nations has been involved in the fight against organized crime from the inception of the organization in 1945, seeking its mandate for this activity in Article 1 of the UN Charter and Article 28 of the Declaration on Human Rights. From the very beginning, the United Nations interpreted organized crime as a threat to the social and economic well-being of the world's population and, quite rightly, concentrated on the purely commercial aspect, taking it to be the core of organized crime—crime as business and crime in business.

The United Nations conventions against crime, including drug trafficking, are crucial in today's world where increased speed of communications and ease of transportation increasingly place judicial authorities in situations involving intractable practical and juridical difficulties. Major criminal cases already pose serious problems on a purely national level, and can become extremely complex when one has to deal with different criminal laws and different legal systems.

The work of the United Nations has, politically, been rather difficult in the area of transnational crime, due in particular to the centrality of the criminal law to the concept of sovereignty. Estella Baker notes rightly that the legitimacy of the state reposes on what she terms a "classical triad": the provision of security, economic well-being, and cultural identity.[12] Criminal law is a core element in the first, plays an important role in the second by keeping the market place clean, and is of import also in the third, as cultural identity is linked to borders and limits. It is therefore less than surprising that states guard their criminal law with some jealousy as crucial to the expression of their legitimacy and in some way of their very identity *qua* states.

Enforcement and technology

Contrary to the relative lack of success in many areas, in particular in so-called "sex tourism," in the area of child pornography on the Internet, adequate use of communication, data storage, and encryption technology can be of value to law enforcement, just as it can be and has been used by violators to transmit, store, and conceal such depictions. Law enforcement has developed new technology in order to penetrate the electronic defenses created to conceal the dissemination and storage of child pornographic material. This dual development and use of modern technology should not surprise, since it really is only an example of the sword–shield syndrome: A stronger sword inevitably leads to a stronger shield, and vice versa. The following two examples emphasize this point.

By surveillance of the Internet using a sniffer-type software, French police from 7–12 October 2007 arrested 310 men aged from 18–70 years for possession of pedo-pornographic images. A total of 1,400,000 photos and 27 videos were seized.

A new initiative launched by the Secretary-General of Interpol in October 2007 is a case in point.[13] A well known, but non-identified pedophile, known under the code name "Vico," had disseminated some 200 photos of himself performing sexual acts with 12 different boys, apparently aged from 6 years to pubescence. The photos, believed to have been made in Vietnam and Cambodia between roughly 2000 and 2003, had been available on the Internet for several years, but "Vico" could not be identified since he had digitally covered his face. The figure covering his face was a cyclone, the vortex of which was constituted by his right eye, perhaps intimating "I see you, you do not see me." In a cooperative effort between Interpol's General Secretariat in Lyons and the German federal police, the Bundeskriminalamt (BKA), the latter succeeded in decrypting the digital face cover and restore the image of the person. On 9 October 2007, Interpol's General Secretariat took the unprecedented step of publishing the restored photograph on the organization's web site in an attempt to identify and locate him. The person in question was quickly identified by several independent sources as being one Christopher Paul Neil, Canadian national, 32 years of age, who earned his living teaching English in South Korea. On 18 October 2007 Interpol issued a Red Notice, which is the equivalent of an international arrest warrant, based on a national arrest warrant issued by Thailand, and the following day, 19 October 2007, he was arrested upon his arrival at Bangkok International Airport. In 2008, he was sentenced to 39 months' imprisonment.

Legislation

In 1988, a most important step forward was taken, namely the adoption of the United Nations Convention against Illicit Traffic in

Narcotic Drugs and Psychotropic Substances, commonly known as the "1988 Vienna Convention." This convention is in many respects a remarkable document, because it introduces a series of international legal innovations, which have been used as models for much subsequent international legislation in this and related areas.[14] It is the first international instrument which in itself acts as an extradition treaty. It introduces the notion of money laundering (without using this term),[15] and provides[16] that if parties require a treaty basis for tracing and freezing of assets, they "shall consider this Convention as the necessary and sufficient treaty basis"; and it lifts bank secrecy.[17] Furthermore, the Convention stipulates that "knowledge, intent or purpose required as an element of the offence [...] may be inferred from objective factual circumstances"[18] and lists among aggravating circumstances (a) the offender belonging to an organized criminal group, and (b) the involvement of the offender in other international organized criminal activities;[19] it furthermore reinforces the *aut dedere aut iudicare* principle.[20] In Article 7 it sets out the requirements for wide-ranging mutual assistance and requires the parties to "Establish and maintain channels of communication between their competent agencies and services ... " It is rare, indeed too rare, for an international legal instrument to make provisions also for international cooperation and enforcement.[21]

The 1994 World Ministerial Conference on Organized Crime in Naples, Italy, of 142 member countries produced the Global Action Plan Against Transnational Organized Crime. Finally, in December 2000, in Palermo, Italy, a Convention on Transnational Organized Crime was opened for signature along with two protocols, the Protocol to Prevent, Suppress and Punish Trafficking in Persons, Especially Woman and Children and the Protocol against the Smuggling of Migrants by Land, Air and Sea. A third protocol, the Protocol against the Illicit Manufacturing of and Trafficking in Firearms, Their Parts and Components and Ammunitions was opened for signature in June 2001. All three protocols supplemented the United Nations Convention against Transnational Organized Crime. A consensus was reached, for the first time, on a definition of trafficking in persons, while the treaty itself enables countries to cooperate even if the crime is not necessarily recognized as such by both countries; the latter often concerns conspiracy charges.

Money laundering

The present section deals with an issue, money laundering, the investigation and interdiction of which over the last 15 years or so have become the foci of much national and international law enforcement. On the present author's view, however, anti-money laundering measures constitute an over-inflated, inefficient, and exceedingly costly tool, in terms both of the monetary cost to society, and of the non-monetary cost in the resultant severe diminution of citizens' privacy rights. The monetary costs of so-called AML (anti-money laundering) measures are dealt with below.

As far as the non-monetary costs are concerned, the main question can be clad in the following terms: It is perhaps the case that so-called money laundering represents a clear criminal danger to society; that being the case, informed citizens may be willing to forego a certain degree of privacy rights in order to establish a transparent banking environment, which might assist law enforcement in elucidating such crime. Nevertheless, it must be considered a sine qua non that the diminution of rights be proportional to the tangible results obtained as a result of such enforcement measures. It is highly dubious if such is the case.

The privacy rights of the population, which have been sacrificed in the imposition of anti-money laundering measures, can perhaps best be summed up by analogy with telephone intercepts. In most countries, law enforcement would not be able to obtain a telephone interception order without being able to show "probable cause" and even so would have difficulties in obtaining a blanket order involving the use by one or more identified persons of a number of clearly identified public telephones.[22] That law enforcement could obtain such an order against unidentified individuals and unidentified public telephones would be inconceivable. That, however, is exactly what the suspicious banking transactions reporting requirement orders banks to do regarding bank accounts. Under these circumstances, it is difficult not to agree with Naylor's judgment that "money laundering is an artificial and contrived offense that has no place in the statute books of a civilized country."[23] Disregarding the natural repugnance one must feel at the idea of turning bank employees into unpaid police informers and the widely exaggerated emphasis on anti-money laundering measures in the so-called fight against terrorist funding, which followed the terrorist acts perpetrated in the United States on 11 September 2001, the question remains, though it has never been adequately answered, of whether the means employed correspond to the results obtained. In this section, a modest attempt will be made to provide a beginning of an answer to just this question.

It is the opinion of the present author that while the present anti-money laundering measures are invasive and inefficient, yet they are also being applied in a manner that is not consistent with their very definition. Masciandaro notes, correctly, that the substantial economic function of money laundering is to transform potential purchasing power into an effective one.[24] Nevertheless, in most jurisdictions defendants are sentenced not for the manipulation of monetary funds in a way suited to conceal their criminal origin and to create "a legend" to explain their origin; instead, they are sentenced for the very transformation of the funds, mostly from cash to real estate. That, however, is not money laundering, as the funds invested in the real estate will still need to be explainable, which they do not become by merely changing their form.

The concept of money laundering sits at the crossroad of three major issues: the accumulation of criminal proceeds, capital flight (KF), and so-called financing of terrorism.[25] The interrelationship between the three issues, and between these and money laundering, can best be illustrated by use of a Venn diagram enhanced by relevant mathematical analysis (Figure 6.1).

In Figure 6.1, the numbers 1–7 indicate the interceptions between the three circles A, B, and C; these are further explicated in tabular form by Table 6.1, below.

It should be noted that the size of the circles and of the areas denominated by the numbers 1 to 7 in Figure 6.1 makes no attempt at proportionality. The Venn diagram in Figure 6.1 does, however, clearly demonstrate the taxonomical complexities one encounters, when

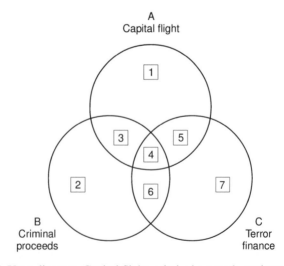

Figure 6.1 Venn diagram. Capital flight, criminal proceeds, and terror finance
Source: Present author.

Table 6.1 Tripartite origin of funds

Row No.	Venn No.	Set Theory Intersections	Explanation
1		U	Monetary funds of non-declared origin in the world
2	1+3+ 4+5	A	Funds resulting from capital flight (KF)
3	2+3+ 4+6	B	Funds of criminal origin
4	4+5+ 6+7	C	Funds used for or destined to be used for the financing of terrorism (CTF)
5	3+4	$A \cap B$	Funds resulting from capital flight, which are of criminal origin, e.g. corruption
6	4+5	$A \cap C$	That part of the financing of terrorism, which originates from capital flight
7	4+6	$B \cap C$	Funds of criminal origin used for the financing of terrorism
8	4	$A \cap B \cap C$	That part of capital flight that is of criminal origin and which is used for the financing of terrorism
9	5	$A \cap -B \cap C$	That part of capital flight that is not of criminal origin, but which is used for the financing of terrorism
10	1	$A \cap -B \cap -C$	Capital flight that is not of criminal origin and which is not used for the financing of terrorism
11	2	$B \cap -A \cap -C$	Funds of criminal origin that do not result from capital flight and which are not used for the financing of terrorism
12	7	$C \cap -A \cap -B$	Funds used for the financing of terrorism, but that are neither of criminal origin not the result of capital flight, e.g. funds funneled thorough the *zakat* structures (charity)
13	3	$A \cap B \cap -C$	Funds from capital flight that are of criminal origin but which are not used for the financing of terrorism
14	6	$B \cap C \cap -A$	Funds of criminal origin that are used for the financing of terrorism, but which are not the result of capital flight

Source: Present author

attempting to determine if monies are of criminal origin, or the result of capital flight, or to be used for the financing of terrorism, or concurrently several of these. Using the symbols commonly employed in set theory, Table 6.1 sets out nine of the possible, context-relevant intersections, all of which have readily observable implications for any law enforcement evaluation of the funds under discussion.[26]

Money laundering has—somewhat narrowly—been characterized by *The Economist* as "the processing through the banking system of the proceeds of crime, in order to disguise their illegal origin."[27] By way of generalization, money laundering is commonly considered a cycle consisting of three stages: placement, layering, and integration. Like all generalizations, this is not always correct since in some cases, there is an overlap between two of the three steps or, occasionally, the whole process only consists of two steps, which happens when two of the three steps are fused into one. The Board of Governors of the Federal Reserve System in the United States explains the terms in the following way:[28]

> The first stage of the process is placement. The placement stage involves the physical movement of currency or other funds derived from illegal activities to a place or into a form that is less suspicious to law enforcement authorities and more convenient to the criminal. The proceeds are introduced into traditional or non-traditional financial institutions or into the retail economy. The second stage is layering. The layering stage involves the separation of proceeds from their illegal source by using multiple complex financial transactions (including wire transfers, monetary instruments) to obscure the audit trail and hide the proceeds The third stage in the money laundering process is integration. During the integration stage, illegal proceeds are converted into apparently legitimate business earnings through normal financial or commercial operations.

Figure 6.2 is a graphic representation, adapted from Pierre Kopp,[29] of two of the money laundering steps, layering and integration. The figure is on three levels, the most important of these being the top level. In two quadrants of the usual Cartesian coordinate system, the equivalent of the y (vertical) axis indicates "transaction costs," while the x (horizontal) axis represents the level of complexity of the money laundering typology. The left quadrant is the layering quadrant, that on the right the integration quadrant. In the first, the layering quadrant, the further one travels to the left and therefore the larger the negative x value, the less complex the methodology; in the right quadrant, the further one is situated to the right and the larger the positive x becomes, the more complex the integration typology used. Transaction costs increase as one travels up the y-axis. Placed within these Cartesian coordinates is a selection of money laundering methodologies, so-called typologies, and their transaction costs in terms of their complexity.

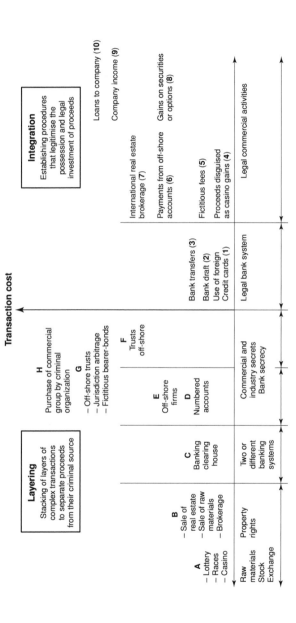

Figure 6.2 Layering and integration
Source: Pierre Kopp, *Délinquances économiques et financières transnationales* (Paris: Institut des Hautes Etudes de Sécurité Intérieure, 2002).

The United States

It is generally agreed that the impetus for the creation of anti-money laundering measures originated in the United States, whence it spread—partially under pressure from the United States—to the rest of the world. Two legislative approaches have in particular marked the fight in the United States against transnational organized crime, namely RICO and the various anti-money laundering provisions enacted in the country since the Bank Secrecy Act of 1970.

The origins of anti-money laundering thinking are to be found in the United States, where as early as the 1960s the idea of depriving the criminals of the proceeds of their crimes took root. The necessary legislation to do so already existed in the various seizure and forfeiture provisions at state and federal level, which allowed law enforcement authorities to seize and later, for the judicial authorities, to order the confiscation or forfeiture of assets originating from crime. The idea, however, slowly emerged to make certain types of investment of funds of illegal origin—as well as the very concealment of the origin of such funds—illegal in themselves. The novelty of so-called anti-money laundering measures in reality consists only in the criminalization of the attempt to conceal the origin of the funds concerned by a number of often otherwise legitimate actions, such as investment in real estate, bank transfers, etc. The concomitant novelty was that much of the effort was to be carried out, and the cost borne by, the private sector. Wolfgang Reinicke[30] developed the term *horizontal subsidiarity* to describe this new process of increasingly assigning and delegating information and analysis responsibilities to the private sector.

It is perhaps no coincidence that the United States already had obtained the sentencing of a major, if not *the* major crime figure of the time, Alphonse Gabriel Capone (1899–1947), not for the crimes which had so much upset public opinion, such as the 1929 Saint Valentine's Day Massacre, but for tax evasion. Levi argues, very credibly, that "Relatively trivial events can be used for tactical reasons against major offenders simply because they are the most serious offences with demonstrable connections to the targets. Al Capone's conviction for tax evasion was merely one early example."[31] One could obviously argue that if the legal system in a country has to have recourse to such indirect approaches in cases concerning major crime, then one should closely examine and overhaul the justice system, including criminal justice legislation and procedure, and law enforcement efficiency, rather than engaging in invasive and ultimately inefficient legislative efforts. However that may be—and it is realized that any judgment of the appropriateness of anti-money laundering legislation to a large degree is dependent on one's view of society[32]—it was natural that the ideas underlying such legislation should develop in the United States, which for years had associated the application of *in rem* civil forfeiture to criminal cases. The underlying basis was that

> When the government institutes proceedings *in rem* for the forfeiture of property involved in criminal proceedings, the Double Jeopardy Clause does not apply so long as the forfeiture proceeding is civil rather than criminal and the forfeiture is not part of the punishment for the criminal offense.[33]

The legislative basis for the U.S. anti-money laundering regime commenced with the 1970 Bank Secrecy Act, while the U.S. 1986 Money Laundering Control Act was the world's first law explicitly directed at money laundering. The Act makes it a crime for a person knowingly to engage in a financial transaction involving the proceeds of a "specified unlawful activity,"[34] while the 1992 Annunzio-Wylie Anti-Money Laundering Act allows for the closure of a bank that has engaged in or allowed money laundering. On 26 October 2001, as Title III of the U.S. Patriot Act, the International Money Laundering Abatement and Financial Anti-Terrorism Act of 2001 was signed into law. This act made changes in the fight against money laundering, in particular by setting new conditions to do business in the United States for foreign financial institutions with assets in the United States, in order to "close certain loopholes whereby US financial institutions were caught up in unscrupulous overseas practices" (*sic*).[35] One of the core provisions in the Act, section 319(a), states that funds deposited at a foreign financial institution that maintains an interbank account[36] in the United States are deemed to have been deposited in the U.S. interbank account with the "covered institution" and can be subject to forfeiture as if they were in the United States.[37] A "covered institution" is, in summary form, any insured bank in the United States, as defined under section 3 (h) of the Federal Deposit Insurance Act, a commercial bank or trust company, a private banker, an agency or branch of a foreign bank in the United States, a credit union, a thrift institution, or a broker or dealer registered with the Securities and Exchange Commission under the Securities Exchange Act of 1934.

As of 2002, a large number of institutions were subject to reporting requirements: 24,000 depository institutions; 160,000 money service businesses; 40,000 U.S. Post Office sites; 600 casinos; 5,000 securities firms; and an undetermined number of other institutions such as insurance companies.[38]

Keeping in mind a narrow view of money laundering as the proceeds of crime processing through the banking system, the question of liability of the banking community, in particular in the United States, remains posed. The February 2001 investigation by the Permanent Subcommittee on Investigations of the U.S. Senate's Committee on Governmental Affairs (in the following "the 2001 Levin Report") estimated that U.S. banks condoned or actively participated in the laundering of more than $250 billion per year, "primarily from drug trafficking and organized crime." The Celent Communications LLC group (a Boston-based financial research company) in a report of September 2003 stated that internationally, money laundering through banks had increased over the preceding four years and for 2004 was projected to reach $424 billion.[39] It is, however, doubtful if major banks will be charged, as noted by Jack Blum:[40] "The money center banks are beyond regulation. There's no capacity to regulate or punish them because they're too big to be threatened with failure." A case in point is the Beacon Hill prosecution[41] conducted by Robert Morgenthau, Manhattan District Attorney, in which on 4 February 2003, a small financial company, Beacon Hill, operating out of rented offices in Manhattan, was the subject of a search warrant. Beacon Hill wired monetary funds in and out of the United States for its clients and by the time it went out of business, the day after the search of its premises, it had wire-transferred $6.5 billion through three dozen accounts it held with J. P. Morgan Chase & Co. According to the prosecutorial authorities,[42] the monetary funds transferred in and out of the United States consisted partly of funds moved out of the United States for tax evasion, and partly of the proceeds of political corruption, including bribes, being moved out of Brazil and into the United States. Beacon Hill was indicted by a New York grand jury for receiving and transmitting money without a New York State Banking Department license. J. P. Morgan Chase was not charged with any crime.

The argument for being lenient on major banks which violate anti-money laundering or, indeed, other provisions, could well be the quite rational fear that such governmental action against major financial institutions might create panic among investors, which would entail turmoil in world financial markets. Finally, in connection with the transfers by illegal Brazilian money transmitters, referred to above, further inquiries showed large unreported flows from offshore accounts in Panama and the Virgin Islands through Bank of America accounts. In late September 2006, Bank of America settled with the New York County District Attorney's office for having allowed Valley National Bank to use 39 accounts with Bank of America to launder $3.7 billion from February 1998 to June 2002. Bank of America paid the City and State of New York $3 million plus $1.5 million in costs, a total of $4.5 million.[43] It is not easy to gauge the gains that Bank of America might have made in allowing the money laundering to take place, but one would guess that it is a lot more than the fine plus costs, 0.12 percent of illegally transferred funds, which the bank, furthermore, had been able to invest gainfully, for instance on the money market, for shorter or longer periods. In other words, the fine plus costs imposed by the court are most certainly considerably less than the fees, commissions, and investment income the bank collected.

The above is another example of deviant knowledge, where in this case the prosecutorial authorities lead the population to believe that a penalty has been imposed, when in reality only a minor part of the fees and commissions collected by a series of illegal operations has been recuperated.

In the Autumn of 1999, the issue of *correspondent banks* came to the fore when the Bank of New York was discovered to be a conduit for billions of dollars of suspect Russian money in the so-called Benex scandal, in which a total of $4.2 billion, believed to be linked to Russian organized crime, passed through a correspondent bank account at the Bank of New York[44] (later reports, however, put this number at $10 billion or even higher), see *US v. Berlin and Edwards*. In this particular case, a couple of computers were housed at an unregistered money-transmission business with full access to the Bank of New York's international wire-transfer service, and unregulated financial institutions in Nauru, with no physical presence anywhere, were used successfully to conceal the real ownership of the laundered funds.[45]

A correspondent bank, as the name indicates, is a bank that opens a bank account in another bank, typically in another jurisdiction. Such correspondent bank accounts are vital to the well-functioning of the international banking system. Thus, the 2001 Levin Report found that as of mid-1999, the five American banks with most correspondent accounts held $17 billion of assets in those accounts, and the top 75 banks held $75 billion. The problem surrounding correspondent bank accounts such as those documented above—in a money laundering context—arises because some of the overseas banks operating correspondent bank accounts in, say, the United States, may be banks that are not under appropriate banking supervision or, indeed, they may not exist or may use a conduit which does not exist. Often the technique of "nesting" is used; this consists in a foreign bank opening an account at another foreign bank, which has a correspondent relationship with, say, an American bank.

In summary of this subsection, it appears to be clear that one of the main themes running through this book, deviant knowledge, is extant even in the regulation of the banking community in the country which has established some of the most stringent banking supervision mechanisms, the United States of America. This is the case when the regulated subject belongs to the very narrow group of banking institutions, the mere hint of instability of which may lead to unrest on the international financial markets.

Taking a global view, Levi notes euphemistically that "Levels of visible enforcement of antilaundering provisions—prosecutions or deauthorizations of financial and professional intermediaries for money laundering or failing to institute proper measures of regulation—have been extremely modest."[46]

The international scene

One might take July 1989 as the crucial date for the imposition of anti-money laundering measures at an international level. In July 1989, at the G7 Arche Summit in France, the G7 began an in-depth treatment of the question of money laundering and, in cooperation with the members of the Organisation for Economic Co-operation and Development (OECD), the G7 developed a series of projects and recommendations. Among the former was the creation of the Financial Action Task Force (FATF), which took place in May 1990; among the latter a set of recommendations which were later issued under the auspices of FATF, the so-called Forty Recommendations.[47] The core proposal and the most transformative policy change, at international level, encompassed the general emphasis on the active participation by financial institutions in the fight against money laundering by spontaneous transfer of data to state institutions of a non-repressive character. In other words, banks had to transfer financial data, hitherto thought to belong to the individual banks and to the individual customers, to a government institution, albeit in most countries non-repressive. This institution would serve as a filter between the banking community and the repressive authorities, and it would pass on to the latter only such information as was deemed necessary, but not necessarily sufficient (as further investigative steps might have to be taken) for prosecution.[48] These institutions were created in many, if not most, countries and, although they are known under various denominations in different countries, they are generically called Financial Intelligence Units (FIUs). The FATF works out of offices in the OECD building in Paris, but is not part of the OECD, while the FIUs are located in the individual member countries. The coordinating unit of the FIUs (the "FIU cooperation council"), known as the Egmont Group of Financial Investigation Units, created 1995, has a secretariat, which for some time and on an temporary basis was run by the NCIS in London, but which, as of the spring of 2007, was established permanently in Toronto; the Group has only FIUs as members, at present 106.[49] One might be forgiven if one were to believe that this impressive array of money laundering fighting institutions was sufficient, but one would be wrong. Between the country level FIU and the overarching, international Egmont Group and the FATF itself, a string of regional organizations have seen the light of day, concurrently creating a number of rather bewildering acronyms: Asia/Pacific Group on Money Laundering (APG); Caribbean Financial Action Task Force on Money Laundering (CFATF); Eastern and Southern Africa Anti-Money Laundering Group (ESAAMLG); Financial Action Task Force of South America (GAFISUD); Middle East and North Africa Financial Task Force (MENAFATF);[50] and the Eurasian Group on Combating Money Laundering and Financing of Terrorism (EAG).[51]

These regional groupings collect and disseminate case histories, trends, and typologies, since such information may very well be urgently needed on a regional basis, rather than awaiting a dissemination on international level. They also examine how FATF recommendations can be best implemented considering the specificities of each region. Finally, in accordance with the Forty Recommendations of the FATF, they perform mutual evaluations of AML/CTF within a regional framework. An example is the February 2007 evaluation by the EAG of Kyrgyzstan. The mutual evaluation[52] was based on the Forty Recommendations 2003 and the Nine Special Recommendations on Terrorist Financing 2002 and 2004[53] of the FATF using the AML/CTF Methodology 2004 as updated in June 2006. It should be noted, however, that the FATF and regional institutions' mandate to organize mutual evaluation studies only extends to the evaluation of the establishment of laws and structures, not to enforcement. One discerns a clear regulatory deficiency in this approach, the results of which are very clear when one examines the efficiency of the AML regime and, in a different area, the lack of enforcement of international legislation on the commercial sexual exploitation of children (CSEC). A rather convincing argument strengthening this deficiency can be adduced from the FATF criteria for defining a country or a territory as "non-cooperative." These criteria are all regulatory and no emphasis seems to be placed on the actual enforcement of such regulations.[54]

A part, but from a money laundering point of view not necessarily the most important part, of the international scene is constituted by so-called offshore centers, which, in summary form, provide two services, (i) banking services, and (ii) corporate services, including a relatively uncomplicated incorporation procedure, as well as tax-free or lenient tax systems. A 1998 survey showed that there were approximately 4,000 offshore banks licensed by nearly 60 offshore jurisdictions. These offshore banks controlled some $5 trillion in assets and were located regionally as follows: Caribbean and Latin America 44 percent, Europe 28 percent, Asia 18 percent, and Middle East and Africa 10 percent.[55]

AML: the cost

As noted in the introduction to this chapter, AML/CTF measures have a very serious cost in terms both of diminution of private rights and of monetary costs. In this subsection only the monetary cost will be considered.

Quantitative information on the costs of AML regime is sparse, but Reuter and Truman arrive at an estimate for the United States for 2003 of approximately $7 billion or about $25 per capita per year.[56] The monetary costs of AML/CTF can conveniently be subdivided into three groups; first, costs supported by the public sector in establishing and administering the regime; second, costs supported by private industry and commerce in carrying out the requirements of the government; and, finally, costs to society as such. The costs absorbed by the general public are transaction costs (for example more documents to be produced), opportunity costs (mostly caused by delays), and compliance costs (loss of privacy may decide some fully law-abiding citizens not to use the banking system rather than being subjected to what they, perhaps quite rightly, see as an intolerable invasion of their privacy). As Reuter and Truman point out, part of the compliance costs arise when the public discovers that the AML requirements are being applied more harshly to individuals than to corporations.[57] Besides, World Bank research from 2004 shows that more regulation in general is associated with lower labor productivity, greater use of the informal economy, increased corruption, and higher costs.[58]

The U.S. government estimates that 2–3 percent of total US expenditures on prevention and enforcement are attributable to the AML regime. For 2004 (in 1995 constant dollars), US federal expenditures to prevention and enforcement were, respectively, $39 and $2.8 billion or a total of $41.8 billion. Taking the higher estimate or 3 percent of total expenditures, one arrives at a U.S. federal cost of AML regulations of $1.25 billion. Added to this should be state- and local-level expenditures, which may exceed the federal level. One therefore arrives at a government spending figure on AML regulations of, at the most, $3 billion.

Few studies are available that estimate the cost to the private sector. For example the KPMG 2003 study for the United Kingdom estimates the cost of U.K. SARs alone to £90 million. Converting this estimate into U.S. dollars and scaling it up for the U.S. economy, one arrives at $1.1 billon, keeping in mind that this only covers the cost of SAR reporting, which is but one element in the AML regime. Studies by PriceWaterhouse Coopers (2003) for the United Kingdom (scaled up to match the United States) and Celent Communications for the United States, arrive respectively at $2.1 and $3.5 billion for total costs. Again, as an estimate, one might claim that costs to the private sector are approximately the same as those to the government, namely $3 billion.

Finally, as regards the costs to the public, Reuter and Truman estimate that financial institutions are capable of passing on approximately one-third of the costs to their customers, i.e. $1 billion, and that a similar amount is absorbed by the public. In summary therefore, total yearly AML costs in the United States are approximately $7 billion.

It is difficult to calculate the costs accruing to the rest of the world, as these are dependent on the degree of AML/CTF measures that each individual jurisdiction has decided to adopt. Nevertheless, as least as a thought experiment—although in the author's view the result is believable—one can make a first estimate by scaling up from the U.S. cost to OECD cost, that is by multiplying the U.S. estimate with the ratio between the OECD GDP and the U.S. GDP (34013/12428.5). For 2005 this is $7 billion multiplied by 2.74, and one thus arrives at the not inconsequential yearly cost of OECD anti-money laundering arrangements of approximately $19.2 billion.

AML: effectiveness

Discussing the effectiveness of anti-money laundering measures, R. T. Naylor notes that "[T]here is not a shred of evidence that the increasingly intrusive and expensive protective measures intended to combat the supposed menace are effective or even necessary."[59]

Judging the effectiveness of the anti-money laundering regime is a subjective matter, since there are no commonly accepted criteria available for determining what characterizes success or its opposite. Nevertheless, information about funds seized and forfeited is available for some countries; it is harder to find information with which to compare such seizures. For the United States, information is available for the year 2001, in which total seizures and forfeitures in money laundering cases totaled $627 million: $386 million in seizures and $241 million forfeitures.[60] If one accepts the lower estimate for money laundering in the United States at $300 billion,[61] then the total seizures and forfeitures represent 0.2 percent of the totality of laundered funds and 9 percent of total costs of the AML regime. The government also levied fines and restitution penalties in the same cases of $665 million. If one were to include these monetary penalties in the seizures and forfeitures, which they are not, one arrives at $1.292 billion or 0.4 percent of the alleged total funds laundered. From a cost analysis point of view, the total amount recovered by the government, $1.292 billion, would then represent 19 percent of total AML costs.

Reuter and Truman[62] argue that if the total amount of funds laundered in the United States in the form of "money laundering of greatest social concern are only a few tens of billions," then the level of penalties (seizures, fines, and restitution) might be 1–3 percent, "perhaps enough to have a modest deterrent effect on those tempted to commit the predicate crimes."

In the 12-year period from 1987–98, according to a KPMG 2003 study, in England and Wales there were only 357 prosecutions for violations of money laundering statutes.[63] A 2003 IMF study found that although the United Kingdom had enacted the laws and put in place the necessary structures, enforcement of the money laundering laws was very limited. A U.K. Cabinet Office study also reached this conclusion, since for 1998 for non-drugs crimes, 136 confiscations were ordered for a total of £22.3 million, of which £10.5 million was collected. In drug cases, some £4.4 million was forfeited, which is a rather modest result, considering that the yearly sale of narcotic drugs in the United Kingdom is estimated at several billion pounds.[64] A further indication of the lack of effectiveness of the "follow the money" methodology is provided by the U.K. Assets Recovery Agency, ARA. The agency was set up in 2003 (with much media attention) and was closed in April 2007. When ARA was set up, it was meant to recuperate some £60 million per year in assets from organized crime, to do which it was provided with unique powers to launch civil recovery proceedings. In the almost four years that the agency operated before closure, it had cost £90 million in running costs, but had not lived up to its recovery targets. Thus, for the year 2004–5, when ARA had cost £20 million to run, it had only recovered some £4.4 million or 22 percent of its own running costs.[65]

Case study: HSBC and the Emirates

Over the last ten years, the United Arab Emirates have emerged as an offshore tax haven whose facilities are attractive to a number of individuals and groups who use them to launder the proceeds of their illegal activities. Here, a specific case involving the use, by Russian nationals, of Hong Kong and Shanghai Banking Corporation (HSBC) banking facilities in the United Arab Emirates will be considered.[66] The case study was chosen because it illustrates three issues of import: first, the presence of Russian nationals in transnational money laundering; second, the not particularly sophisticated methodology used; and, finally, the responsibility of the banking community, be the banks' actions or inactions based on willful blindness, knowing involvement, or corruption.

Information obtained by the Central Bank of the UAE in 2000 indicated that certain financial movements within the HSBC were parts of a massive money laundering operation and that a number of local HSBC executives would appear to have been guilty of "passive complicity" in the money laundering operations. A review of two years' activities of the HSBC disclosed irregularities in two of HSBC's branches, respectively in Sharjah and Deira.[67] The summary conclusions were that the turnover on Russian accounts in the two branches over the two years examined were "indicative of money laundering on a massive scale," while management at the two branches "failed to observe their internal policy guidelines with regard to 'Know Your Customer' (KYC) and review of the daily large transactions report," and that incoming remittances on some of the accounts were incommensurate with the level of disclosed income of account holders. The summary conclusion of the review was that:

> The Bank is not following our instructions contained in the Circular No. 163/98 dated 28/02/1998 concerning unusual transactions in an account. They did not report to the Central Bank details of such accounts involving dubious transactions. They also quietly closed some accounts involving money laundering and did not report them to the Central Bank.[68]

The Central Bank examiners found that in 2000, despite closing a number of Russian HSBC accounts in the UAE, there were a total of 1,186 such HSBC accounts, with a total deposit base of AED125.3 million ($34.2 million).[69] Even a cursory look at the bank reveals that of the bank's eight branch offices in the United Arab Emirates, two, the Deira and Sharjah branches, had opened 927 of the total 1,186 HSBC accounts in the country (78.2 percent) with deposits of AED111.3

million of total deposits in the country of AED125.3 (88.8 percent.) The very penetrability of only a couple of branch offices should have alerted supervisory management to the strong possibility of corruption. Also, the UAE Central Bank examiners noted that in the cases where HSBC did close down accounts, the balance on the accounts was paid to the account holders in the form of banker's checks, which admittedly allowed these individuals to re-start the money laundering cycle elsewhere with the least possible obstacles.

It should also strike a responsible bank officer that the accounts displayed unusual movement patterns. Thus, 40.5 percent of deposits were effectuated via inward telegraphic transfers and 53.7 percent from transfers from other accounts in the bank. Withdrawals were equally remarkable: 31.8 percent in cash, 19.7 percent in outward telegraphic transfers, and 37.7 percent by transfer to other accounts in the bank.[70]

Even the simplest due diligence and "know your customer" inquiries should have generated concern. By way of examples, an individual, K. M., declared a monthly income of AED3,000, but over two years deposited AED6 million; 94 percent by inward telegraphic transfers, as were all withdrawals. S. A. G. Trading opened an account, deposited AED22.1 million by telegraphic transfer, and on the same day transferred the same amount outwards, also telegraphically. These unexplained transactions did not spur HSBC to investigate the account holders.

It can be taken for granted that one is here in the presence of part of stage two of the money laundering cycle, layering. The disparity between the number of Russian accounts, their balances in the various HSBC branches throughout the UAE, and the use, on those accounts, of inward and outward telegraphic transfers would have been easily detectable using a not very sophisticated computer software program.

A question that has often been brought up is that of the degree of responsibility, either direct knowledge or willful blindness, that one must allot to the bank in which the accounts were held, one of the largest banks in the world, HSBC. Considering the size and sophistication of HSBC's worldwide operations, it is difficult to believe that the bank was not in possession of the management tools, the experience, and the technological expertise necessary to detect the quite obvious money laundering-oriented banking patterns that emerge from even a cursory look at the bank's records.

Case study: Thailand's AMLO

In Thailand, the laundering of criminal proceeds is deemed to pose a threat both to the kingdom's financial stability and to national security.[71] The Thai Anti-Money Laundering Act[72] of B.E.[73] 2542 (1999) became effective on 19 August 1999.[74] The Act criminalizes "the act of money laundering and related conspiracy, creates [and] establishes a civil forfeiture system for confiscating assets identified as having been acquired with the proceeds of specific predicate criminal offences and creates an Office of Anti-Money Laundering."[75] Thailand has chosen a thematic rather than a generic approach to establishing what constitutes predicate offences, and in section 3 of the Act enumerates these: narcotic offences (§1); sexual offences in particular procurement of women and children (§2); fraud (§3); securities offences (§4); corruption (§5); extortion or blackmail by "member of an unlawful secret society or organized criminal association" (§6); customs evasion (§7); offences related to terrorism (§8). The latter was enacted to comply with UN resolution 1373 by the Amendment to the Penal Code Section 135; it became effective on 11 August 2003.

In section 13 of the Act, Thailand established a suspicious transactions reporting requirement; it is noteworthy that, in section 3 of the Act, the Thai legislator includes in the definition of suspicious transaction the characteristic of "a transaction that is more complicated than the norm by which that transaction is usually conducted, a transaction that lacks economic rationale."[76] Section 15 of the Act enjoins the Land Office with a reporting responsibility regarding trade in immovable assets and section 16 obliges the owner of an investment business to report investment transactions. Finally, section 20 of the Act establishes a customer due diligence (CDD) regime.

In consequence of Thailand's adherence to the 1988 Vienna Convention, the Office of the Narcotics Control Board (ONCB),[77] under the leadership of Pol. Gen. Chaovalit Yodmanni, then the Secretary-General of ONCB, had drawn up the first draft law criminalizing conspiracy, which to some degree permitted the seizure of funds originating from the illicit traffic in narcotic substances, the so-called Conspiracy Act, enacted in Thailand in 1991.

The not inconsequential disadvantage of using a thematic rather than a generic approach to identifying the underlying, so-called predicate crimes is obvious in the case of Thailand, but by no means only Thailand, namely that crimes, which in some way obstruct or undermine the interests of the ruling elite can easily be excluded from the listing. Among such excluded crimes one finds currency exchange offences, smuggling, fraud in financial institutions, labor fraud, excise fraud, gambling and forestry offences.

In April 2000, AMLO became a member of the Asia/Pacific Group on Money Laundering (APG) and in June 2001 of the Egmont Group of Financial Intelligence Units.

The anti-money laundering legislation in Thailand, as in many other countries, is being used, not really to suppress money laundering, but simply as a further weapon against criminals, whereby their assets, which for evidentiary or other reasons could not be forfeited under the 1991 Conspiracy Act, are seized in a civil lawsuit by the AMLO. The Act has, embedded in it, a strange contradiction: section 3 §2 of the Act does not allow for the Act to be used in cases of smuggling of persons (trafficking in humans), unless the reason for the smuggling is sexual exploitation; this contradiction is presumably due to an oversight in the drafting phase.

This chapter has examined the various initiatives against transnational organized crime; in particular it has questioned the basis for and enforcement of anti-money laundering measures. The following chapter will continue this strand of thought by considering some of the contemporary critical issues in the study of the subject-matter, and will attempt to identify some of the future crimes by which transnational organized crime will maintain its income-flow.

7 Critical issues and future trends

Albeit with a pinch of pessimism, one cannot but agree with Jeffrey Robinson's proposition that

> As long as we live in a world where a seventeenth-century philosophy of sovereignty is reinforced with an eighteenth-century judicial model, defended by a nineteenth-century concept of law enforcement that is still trying to come to terms with twentieth-century technology, the twenty-first century will belong to transnational crime.[1]

His criticism, however, should be extended to philosophers, legislators, and law enforcement officials alike, but should also be aimed at scholars. If scholarship continues to be immersed in rather introspective definitional quarrels, it is not doing very well in fulfilling its advisory role.

Although rejected by some scholars, the authoritative 2000 CATOC definition of transnational organized crime is now available and in order to make important advances in this area of study, it should be taken as the accepted standard. Likewise, scholars would advance both learning and praxis considerably if they were to apply "differential diagnosis" to terrorism instead of insisting on having one, vague category termed "terrorism" as a kind of catch-all, which allows the individual scholar to make a selection fitting his or her political standpoint. Thus, "terrorism" along the lines proposed in Chapter 4 should be clearly distinguished from the terror inflicted by a tyrannical ruler on his or her population, as well as from acts of violence perpetrated by agents of a foreign state. Only by refining our tools can we apply more subtle analyses and develop more refined counter-measures.

The enlarged international space occupied and perceived to be occupied by transnational crime (made possible by the deregulation of the financial markets, by increased ease of transportation of persons or goods, and by the truly remarkable developments in communication and data storage capabilities), the opening up of the markets in Eastern Europe, an increased awareness on the political and academic levels[2] of the extent in breadth and depth of the phenomenon, and, lastly, the efforts made by the United Nations and its sister organizations, for example the important analytical work done by the economists at the IMF,[3] constitute the determinants of the transnational crime discourse.

The current debates in the area very much analyze these issues: Is so-called globalization a determining factor in the development of transnational organized crime? Are modern communication capabilities of more import in this context than the invention of the telegraph? Has globalization or the opening of Eastern Europe had the greater impact? And so forth. Most importantly, though, is the necessity to keep measuring the efficacy of the counter-measures applied and to develop the courage to discontinue inefficient ones also against arguments from entrenched bureaucratic quarters.

Developments within well established Italian organized crime groups disclose the strategy that they will adopt at least in the near future: They have established and are establishing cooperative arrangements with Italian and foreign organized crime groups in Italy, and with foreign organized crime groups outside of Italy.[4] There is little doubt that such horizontal networks, exploiting competitive advantages, will occupy much of the future transnational organized crime space.

Countering such networks is notoriously difficult as they display a series of characteristics, which work to ensure their survival, such as non-transparency, flexibility, and self-repair capabilities. It is obvious, but probably utopian to advise governments to dissolve irrelevant and non-enforceable prohibition regimes, to discontinue inefficient, costly and liberticidal enforcement strategies, and to acknowledge the criminogenic effects of excessive revenue and sanction impositions. If, nevertheless, the political choices of the future involve the continuation of the present policies, governments should fully realize a number of unpleasant facts. First, demand in the developed world for the goods and services offered by transnational criminal networks will not diminish, in particular that for prostitution, gambling, drugs, and arms. This unpalatable fact is difficult to explain, but a beginning of an explanation may have been proposed by Walter Lippmann in his 1925 work *The Phantom Public*.[5] Just as Chapter 1 pointed to a certain *societal alienation* between a cosmopolitan elite and the population as such, in the developed world one is also in the presence of a complex form of societal alienation between the governance structures and the general public, namely the Lippmannian "phantom public," as the latter, because of the increasing complexity of socio-political developments, has diminishing ability to comprehend the former.

Second, any enforcement policy can be nothing but palliative; an alleged "interdiction" is an impossibility. It is hardly necessary to elaborate on this point; from Prohibition to the war against drugs, interdiction efforts have failed to eradicate the criminalized behavior. There is no reason to believe that this fact will change in the future; quite to the contrary, ease of transportation as well as the increasing international travel will only make the success of international interdiction efforts even more illusory.

Third, governments should comprehend that norm enforcement is a zero-sum game; funds allocated to irrelevant and ineffective enforcement policies by definition are not available for other enforcement areas. But the core threats to society do not come from drug trafficking or from the way criminals apply their ill-gotten gains. Instead, crimes against the environment and crimes against the human being *qua* human being (neo-slavery, trafficking in humans) represent the clear and present danger.

Finally, if governments persist in the supply reduction direction adopted so far, they should realize that for the fight against transnational criminal networks to reach at least a minimal level of efficiency will demand the kind of capillary intelligence cooperation, based on complexity theory, for which no jurisdiction so far has been prepared.

New transnational crimes

Naím[6] observes that transnational organized crime will continue to expand; its networks are not bound by geography and defy traditional notions of sovereignty. An important part of the present and, more so, future revenues of organized crime will originate from both trafficking in human beings and human smuggling; not only this, but both are fast expanding activities, as individuals from less privileged countries attempt to establish themselves in more economically developed ones. This tendency, however, will most certainly accelerate in the future as climate changes will put even more pressure on less developed countries by impoverishing the already not very rich soil. Everything leads one to believe that this expansion will continue and it will ensure that transnational crime gains access to an ever increasing pool of recruits and victims.

The greatly increased use of trade embargoes and trade sanctions under international law will supply organized crime with ample opportunities for revenue because they will invest their commercial and organizational skills in providing the goods and services which cannot be supplied by legitimate trade. The operative terms here are *denied demand* and *criminogenesis*.

The ageing of the population of the Western world will lead to a whole range of opportunities for organized crime, the most obvious of which is the supply of replacement organs from willing or, if necessary, unwilling donors. The present author put forward the idea of unwilling organ donors as a future crime at several international forums,[7] although it was perceived to be far-fetched. Now, however, the first documented case is available from India, where on 28 January 2008, authorities disclosed a case of trafficking in organs harvested from the poor and sold to rich clients. As reported, hundreds of donors had been ensnared, often with false promises of work, and induced by threat with a weapon to donate one of their kidneys against a payment of $1,250. The kidneys were then resold at ten times this price.[8] In this instance, the donors were left alive, whereas there have been a number of undocumented reports from South America of poor "donors," who were brought in from the street by force, killed, and used for full organ harvesting. Equally, the counterfeiting of high-price cutting-edge pharmaceuticals holds promises of vast earnings for organized crime.

Finally, the involvement of organized crime in environmental abuse, in particular in the disposal of toxic waste, is perceived by some observers as the most profitable future criminal activity of transnational organized crime. Also, the undoubtedly transnational criminal acts connected with the international trade in forest product, which is illegal at source, is worrying.

Italy

Although this book has attempted to avoid an over-reliance on organized crime studies from and about Italy, some recent quantitative data are of particular interest for two reasons. First, they do not originate from government or scholarship, but from a segment of society which typically is the victim of organized crime, namely small and medium-size businesses, represented by their professional association, Confesercenti.[9] Second, the report both analyzes the data and looks at future developments.

The table in Annex 8 contains the data pertaining to the earnings in Italy of organized crime as estimated by Confesercenti based on information from the association's membership. In the table, "The Mafia Co." indicates a virtual holding company that consolidates the balance sheets of the four companies that it controls: the Mafia, the Camorra, the 'ndrangheta, and the Sacra Corona Unita. The biggest of the four is now 'ndrangheta, which, according to the Italian Minister of the Interior, Roberto Maroni, controls the European drugs market and has a yearly profit of €45 billion.[10]

According to Confesercenti, members of the professional association now pay €250 million a day to organized crime in Italy in "protection" and usury. The going "protection"—the *pizzo*—rate is €10,000 per month for a building site, €3–5,000 for a supermarket, and €200–500 for small shops. Also stall owners on markets pay a couple of euros a day and Gypsies €50 a month for their illegal sheds The latter is of import, because it is clear that organized crime does not need, is not interested in a couple of euros a day and a small donation from the Gypsies. I argue that they extort these small amounts as part of an overall strategy to make clear to all and sundry who is in charge of the territory. The report, however, also points out that the association's membership, because it is constituted by small and medium-size businesses, is the most vulnerable to a lack of liquidity in the financial markets and that therefore in any financial crisis, its members have no other access to credit than via organized crime usurers. A total of 180,000 members had reported to their professional association to have done so, and more undoubtedly will have to do so in any period of economic downturn. This is but another example of denied demand, which is being satisfied.

As noted earlier in this chapter, cooperation between Italian organized crime and foreign criminal organizations definitely is a trend, which, in my view, will become of great import in the future. It is, however, also worth noticing the flexibility of organized crime, which, as just outlined, in economically difficult periods can adjust itself to the new circumstances and engage in or further develop the criminal activity which is best suited; in the present situation, usury.

New institutional counter-measures

Various counter-measures have been undertaken on the international level, both within the ambit of the United Nations and by intergovernmental organizations such as Interpol, and regional institutions, for instance Europol. Such developments, however, come at a price, in particular the already observable militarization of law enforcement and the gradual disappearance of the formal or informal demarcation between internal and external security, as evidenced in the important work of Anthony Giddens, among others. The danger inherent in this evolution is an already clearly observable diminution of civil rights.

In the area of illegal logging, one could obviously ask why ordinary criminal prosecutions for theft, receiving stolen goods, etc., are not undertaken. One answer is provided by the Thai AMLO, who takes the view that the major problem is that "wood is wood" and that it is difficult, not to say impossible, to determine from where wood originates and therefore to trace it back to illegal or illicit origins. AMLO's point of view is understandable considering today's enforcement priorities, but I would argue that this is one precise area where important advances are possible. For this to happen, however, would require that individual countries, regions, and the alleged international community re-prioritize law enforcement objectives.[11] That must mean, in particular, environmental crime, among which illicit and illegal logging must be considered a leading priority.

In the 1970s, U.S., but not only U.S., narcotics law enforcement created central databases, which allowed their users, from the chemical composition of seized narcotic drugs, to identify the place of production—not only the country or region, but also the very laboratory which had effectuated the transformation of, say, opium into morphine base. Without being an expert in forestry or chemistry, I would propose the hypothesis that trees embed in their wood, in the course of their growing, enough markers to determine at least the country and presumably also the region whence they originate. To create a central worldwide database of such markers would provide a very important enforcement tool, which would be of crucial importance in combating illegal logging, including the concomitant money laundering.

8 Conclusion

The first conclusion of this book is that the concept of identity is underdeveloped in the study of organized crime, both with respect to our establishment of an identity for organized crime and regarding its establishment of one for itself. In most countries, there is a (perhaps class-conscious?) reluctance to apply, for example, the UN CATOC definition to crime and talk of organized crime, when one is facing a "structured group of three or more persons, existing for a period of time and acting in concert with the aim of committing one or more serious crimes or offences in order to obtain, directly or indirectly, financial or other material benefit," even if the individuals concerned hold high office and can afford the best legal representation. Likewise, as pointed out in the introduction of the concept of *societal alienation*: Do these individuals realize that they are "organized crime figures"?— to use a popular media term.

The second conclusion of the book basically concerns intellectual probity. Mike Maguire, Rod Morgan, and Robert Reiner (editors of the fourth edition of the authoritative *Oxford Handbook on Criminology*)[1] proclaim that they do not "embrace a fashionable postmodern relativism about truth or justice;" nor does the author of this work. Nevertheless, it is crucial to make it very clear that criminal justice is a zero-sum game; criminal justice budgets in all countries are not infinite and funds that are allocated to one issue or particular strategy are not available for some other issue or strategy. This is obviously also the case for transnational organized crime and even more so, since such crimes are, in general, expensive to investigate because of their overseas links and due to the sophistication of the precautionary measures taken by the individuals involved. It is therefore of crucial importance that funds are well allocated. This implies, at a minimum: First that particular care should be exercised in elaborating criminal justice strategies whose focus is placed on issues that either pose a discernible risk to society as such or, indeed, to humanity or which particularly violate the value-system of the community; and, second, that once programs have been established and activated in accordance with chosen strategies, the cost-benefit of such programs must be constantly monitored and the programs discontinued if inefficient. The long-lasting, exceedingly costly and ineffectual so-called "war on drugs" is a case in point. The equally costly and equally ineffectual money laundering regime is another. These law enforcement programs have by now been running long enough for it to be abundantly clear that they have made no impact of significance, neither on the availability of narcotic drugs, nor on the ability of criminals and, for that matter, terrorists to dispose of their funds when and where they desire.

This leads one to pose a corollary of Durkheim's observation that crime is a normal social fact: one must arrive at the third conclusion, namely that transnational crime is a normal international social fact. Having accepted that, however, one must avoid the Scylla and Charybdis of, on the one hand, an unsubstantiated and undoubtedly erroneous belief in a worldwide Mafia conspiracy and, on the other, an equally misguided state of denial of the present and potential transnational reach of organized crime.

The fourth conclusion one would wish to draw from the book relates to criminogenesis. While one can easily understand that individual governments attempt to claw in duties and taxes they have imposed on individuals or on product, one can legitimately ask to what degree governments themselves have created the tendency to evade such duties. Norms that are seen to be unreasonable and are felt by the population as incongruous with the popular ethical conception which subtends criminal law, as for example the exaggerated revenue-generating import and sales duties on tobacco product, are by their very nature criminogenic, since unreasonable provisions will be tacitly and openly violated by a large proportion of a population. Tobacco product is taxed by a duty many times the value of the product itself; it could be argued that imposing a duty higher than the value of the product itself, in other words de-reifying it, not only is unreasonable, it is a clear invitation to norm disobedience.

Fifth, one could reasonably ask to what degree and by what means governments should investigate violations, in particular revenue evasion. Any law enforcement-type investigation involves, by necessity, an infringement of individual rights to privacy, to freedom, etc. Some might feel that the drastic measures proposed by the World Health Organization (WHO) in the Protocol to the WHO Framework Convention on Tobacco Control by far exceed what is reasonable for an infringement of such revenue regulations; in other words these propositions represent a disproportionate justification for misusing resources and depleting ethics.[2] This protocol proposes a series of enforcement measures which hitherto have only been used in the investigation of drug trafficking and other very serious crimes. Their introduction in this protocol could and should be seen as rather surprising considering that the product which the convention attempts to control is perfectly legal and freely available in all countries in the world. Observing the very substantial legal remedies being put in place in simple cases of violation of revenue regulations, one cannot but point to the far more important subject of commercial sexual exploitation of children. The paltry results obtained, at international level, in this serious area are in stark contrast to the measures proposed when the issue is not the lives of innocent children, but government revenue. Not only should investigative resources be applied in accordance with the opprobrium of the population, but their very implementation in the investigation of revenue violations ultimately will lead to a hollowing-out of the population's sense of justice and—while undoubtedly meant to create governmental income to strengthen society—will ultimately undermine the very society, *qua* society, it alleges to uphold.

The sixth conclusion is that to advance in our understanding of transnational organized crime, we should bear in mind the two aspects or points of view based on scaling theory that I proposed in the Introduction. Hitherto, the very common kinds of street-level crime, for example retail theft or sale of counterfeit goods, have not been appreciated at their full value, because two mutually exclusive approaches have been used. On the one side criminology has taken an interest in the street-level criminal and his or her socio-economic circumstances, while, on the other, international relations scholars have considered the international production and transportation of goods and services, and their implications for that particular field of study. It is crucial, however, that we attempt to understand how these, at first glance so uninteresting, street crimes ultimately explain both employment patterns that are of some complexity and the accrual of substantial profits. Richard Lambert noted that "Borders are little more than a fantasy of foreign ministers" and any naïve belief that we will ever be able to control our national borders again, if indeed we ever were, is just that, naïve.[3]

Finally, and returning to my remarks, above, in the first conclusion, at the time of writing this in the autumn of 2008, the developed world is undergoing a financial crisis which may be the most severe since

1929. The structural instability and the financial volatility which both accompanies and defines the crisis, will, undoubtedly, provide transnational organized crime with new opportunities for gain, from usury to market speculation. It is also, however, a propitious moment in which to reflect on the differences between the underworld and the upperworld, if any.

Annex 1

Table A.1 Number of drugs and substances under international control, 1912–95

	1912	1925	1931	1948	1961	1971	1988	1995
Synthetic	0	0	0	12	53	98	187	245
Natural	4	7	17	24	32	32	33	37
Total	4	7	17	36	85	130	220	282
Natural as % of total	100	100	100	66.7	37.6	24.6	15	13.1

Source: adapted from I. Bayer and H. Ghodse, "The Response: Evolution of International Drug Control 1945–1995." Draft paper for UNDCP, 1996.

Annex 2

Table A.2 Wholesale and retail prices, heroin, Europe and the United States, 1990–2006, U.S.$/g

	Europe		U.S.A.	
Year	*Retail*	*Wholesale*	*Retail*	*Wholesale*
1990	268	144	433	251
1991	221	101	413	229
1992	211	111	385	216
1993	149	76.6	374	304
1994	161	76.7	277	194
1995	158	69.6	259	193
1996	151	61.7	219	182
1997	117	49.6	190	162
1998	117	45.1	200	154
1999	105	41.5	166	129
2000	74.5	33.4	148	95
2001	67.1	29.4	125	67.7
2002	70	31.6	98	56.9
2003	76.8	33.2	127	71.8
2004	80.6	34.5	162	73.4
2005	74	32.9	201	67.1
2006	67.1	30.7	172	87.7

Source: UN Office on Drugs and Crime, *2008 World Drug Report* (Vienna, Austria: UNODC, June 2008), 49.

Annex 3

Table A.3 Narcotics statistics, the United States. Federal costs, U.S.$ millions

FY	2002	2003	2004	2005	2006	2007	2008	2009
Demand	4916.0	4949.2	5122.5	5144.2	4947.6	4902.7	4982.8	4909.8
%	45.6	44.1	42.7	40.2	37.6	35.4	36.5	34.8
Supply	5865.4	6270.9	6883.2	7640.2	8196.4	8941.4	8672.6	9204.6
%	54.4	55.9	57.3	59.8	62.4	64.6	63.5	65.2
Total	10781.4	11220.1	12005.7	12784.4	13144.0	13844.1	13655.4	14114.4

Source: Office of National Drug Control Policy, *National Drug Control Strategy. FY2009. Budget Summary* (Washington, D.C.: The White House, February 2008).

Annex 4

Table A.4 The drug user population

Population	2006–2007 (millions)	%	2004 (millions)	
Total world population	6,475		6389	
World population, 15–64 years of age	4,272	100	4102	100
Non-drug using population, 15–64 years of age	4,064	95.1	3902	95.1
Annual prevalence of drug use (has used drugs at least once within last year), 15–64 years of age	208	4.8	200	4.9
Monthly prevalence of drug use (has used drugs at least once within last month), 15–64 years of age	112	2.6	110	2.7
Problem drug use, 15–62 years of age	26	0.6	25	0.6

Source: UN Office on Drugs and Crime, *2008 World Drug Report* (Vienna, Austria: UNODC, June 2008), 30. UN Office on Drugs and Crime, *2006 World Drug Report* (Vienna, Austria: UNODC, June 2008), 8.

Annex 5

Table A.5 Worldwide seizures of drugs, excluding cannabis (millions of tons)

Product (mt)	2005	2006
Coca leaf	3209	3304
Cocaine	743	705
Opium	342	384
Heroin	58	58
Morphine	32	46
Amphetamine	21	19
Methamphetamine	17	16
Ecstasy	5	4
Methaqualone	1	5
Depressants	1	1

Source: UNODC, *World Drug Report* (Vienna, Austria: UNODC, 2008), 8.

Annex 6

Table *A.6* Seizures of smuggled cigarettes. Europe, 1999 (millions)

United Kingdom	1534
Italy	1395
Spain	1200
Portugal	1071
The Netherlands	256
Belgium	150
Ukraine	122

Source: WCO.

Annex 7

Table A.7 Plastic card fraud losses on U.K.-issued cards, 1997–2007

£ millions							Of which	
Year	Total	CNP	Counter-feit	Lost-stolen	Card ID theft	Mail non-received	U.K. retailer face-to-face	U.K.	Abroad
1997	122	10	20.3	66.2	13.1	12.5	72.2	92.8	29.2
1998	135	13.6	26.8	65.8	16.8	12	74.8	100.1	34.9
1999	188.4	29.3	50.3	79.7	14.4	14.6	93	134.1	54.2
2000	317	72.9	107.1	101.9	17.4	17.7	139.1	213.4	103.5
2001	411.5	95.7	160.4	114	14.6	26.8	188.9	273	138.4
2002	424.6	110.1	148.5	108.3	20.6	37.1	186.9	294.4	130.2
2003	420.4	122.1	110.6	112.4	30.2	45.1	177.9	316.3	104.1
2004	504.8	150.8	129.7	114.5	36.9	72.9	218.8	412.3	92.5
2005	439.4	183.2	96.8	89	30.5	40	135.9	356.6	82.8
2006	427	212.7	98.6	68.5	31.9	15.4	72.1	309.9	117.1
2007	535.2	290.5	144.3	56.2	34.1	10.2	73	327.6	207.6

Source: APACS, *Fraud: The Facts, 2008* (London: APACS, 2008).

Annex 8

Table A.8 The Mafia Co. balance sheet (billions of €)

Actives			Passives		
Illicit Traffics		**66.30**	**Salaries**		**1.76**
*Drugs	59.00		*Heads	0.60	
*Humans	0.30		*Affiliated	1.00	
*Weapons & various	5.80		*Prisoners	0.03	
*Smuggling	1.20		*Fugitives	0.13	
Mafia Taxes		**21.60**	**Logistics**		**0.45**
*Racketeering	9.00		*Safe houses	0.10	
*Usury	12.60		*Networks	0.10	
			*Weapons	0.25	
Predatory Activities		**1.00**			
*Theft, robbery, fraud	1.00		**Corruption Activities**		**3.80**
			*Corruption	1.95	
Entrepreneurial Activities		**24.70**	*Consultants & Specialists	0.05	
*Tenders & supplying	6.50		*Supporters	1.80	
*Agriculture (agromafia)	7.50				
*Gambling	2.40		**Legal Expenses**	0.70	**0.70**
*Counterfeiting	6.30				
*Abusive Building	2.00		**Investments**	30.00	**30.00**
Ecomafia	16.00	**16.00**	**Laundering**	22.50	**22.50**
Prostitution	0.60	**0.60**	**Savings**	7.50	**7.50**
Financial Income	0.75	**0.75**			
Total Actives		**130.95**	**Total Passives**		**66.71**
			Net Profit		**64.24**

Source: Underlying dataset (which has been further analyzed) is from Confesercenti, "Le mani della criminalità sulle imprese. XI Rapporto SOS
Impresa-Confesercenti" (Rome, Italy: Confesercenti, 11 November 2008).

Notes

Foreword

1 See, for example, Peter Romaniuk, *Multilateral Cooperation Against Terrorism* (London: Routledge, forthcoming); and Richard J. Goldstone and Adam M. Smith, *International Judicial Institutions: The Architecture of International Justice at Home and Abroad* (London: Routledge, 2008).
2 Frank G. Madsen, "Organized crime," in *The Oxford Handbook of the United Nations*, ed. Thomas G. Weiss and Sam Daws (Oxford: Oxford University Press, 2007), 611–19.
3 Frank G. Madsen, "Complexity, transnational organised crime and terrorism: Can notions from the edge of chaos help us understand?" Paper read at the International Studies Association Conference, 2 February 2007, Chicago, Illinois.
4 Gennaro Scala, Frank G. Madsen, and Carlo Biffani, "FORUM: Sicurezza energetica: La nuova frontiera dell'Intelligence," *Gnosis* 2 (July 2008): 25–48.

Introduction

1 Frank G. Madsen, *Complexity, Transnational Organised Crime and Terrorism: Can Notions From the Edge of Chaos Help Us Understand?* Paper presented at the International Studies Association (ISA) conference, Chicago, 2 March 2007.
2 Walter Lippmann, "The underworld as servant," in *Organized Crime in America: A Book of Readings*, ed. Gus Tyler (Ann Arbor, Mich.: University of Michigan Press, 1967), 59–69.
3 The subject of organized crime has given rise to heated discussions among scholars, often holding extreme views. For a thorough, well-balanced treatment of the subject, see Michael Levi, "The organization of serious crimes," in *Oxford Handbook of Criminology. 3rd Edition*, ed. Mike Maguire, Rod Morgan, and Robert Reiner (Oxford and New York: Oxford University Press, 2002), 878–913.
4 Peter Andreas, "Transnational crime and economic globalization," in *Transnational Organized Crime and International Security: Business As Usual?* ed. Mats Berdal and Mónica Serrano (Boulder, Colo.: Lynne Rienner, 2002), 39.

1 Taxonomy

1 James W. E. Sheptycki, "Criminology and the transnational condition: A contribution to international political sociology," *International Political Sociology* 1, no. 4 (2007): 391–406.

2 Sheptycki, "Criminology and the transnational condition: A contribution to international political sociology," 393.

3 Charles Tilly, "War making and state making as organized crime," in *Bringing the State Back In*, ed. Peter Evans, Dietrich Rueschemeyer, and Theda Skocpol (Cambridge: Cambridge University Press, 1985), 169–91.

4 This important approach is linked to two books by John Urry, *Sociology Beyond Societies: Mobilities for the Twenty-First Century* (London: Routledge, 2000) and *Global Complexity* (Cambridge: Polity, 2003). See also Stanley Cohen, "Intellectual scepticism and political commitment: The case of radical criminology" in *The New Criminology Revisited*, ed. Paul Walton and Jock Young (London: Macmillan, 1998), 98–129; Nancy Fraser, *Justice Interruptus: Critical Reflections on the Post-Socialist Condition* (New York: Routledge, 1999).

5 Roland Marchal, Fariba Adelkhah, and Sari Hanafi, eds, *Dubaï, cité global* (Paris: CNRS-Editions, 2001). Saskia Sassen, *The Global City: New York, London, Tokyo*, 2nd ed. (Princeton, N.J.: Princeton University Press, 2001).

6 Tom Wolfe, *The Bonfire of the Vanities* (New York: Farrar, Straus, and Giroux, 1987), 73.

7 Felix Geyer, "Political alienation and environmental complexity reduction." Paper prepared for the session on "Political Alienation" at the 12th Annual Scientific Meeting of the International Society of Political Psychology, Tel-Aviv, Israel, 18–23 June 1989, available in *Kybernetes* 19, no. 2 (1990): 11–31.

8 André Bossard, *Transnational Crime and Criminal Law* (Chicago: Office of International Criminal Justice, 1990). André Bossard was Secretary-General of the International Criminal Police Organisation, ICPO, Interpol, at Saint-Cloud, France.

9 Adam Edwards and Peter Gill, eds, *Transnational Organised Crime: Perspectives on Global Security* (London and New York: Routledge, 2006).

10 Carlo Devito, *Encyclopedia of International Organized Crime* (New York: Facts on File, 2005).

11 John M. Martin and Anne T. Romano, *Multinational Crime: Terrorism, Espionage, Drug and Arms Trafficking* (Thousand Oaks, Calif.: Sage Publications, 1992).

12 Terrorism refers to international law in general, while organized crime is "transnational" with reference to the title of the Convention Against Transnational Organized Crime (CATOC) (December 2000).

13 *Sarei v. Rio Tinto* (U.S. Court of Appeals, 9th Circuit, 7 August 2006).

14 James W. E. Sheptycki, "Against transnational organized crime," in *Critical Reflections on Transnational Organized Crime*, ed. Margaret E. Beare (Toronto: Toronto University Press, 2003), 120–44.

15 The United Kingdom seems to have introduced yet another concept, "Serious Organized Crime," in the Serious Organised Crime and Police Act, 2005.

16 Sheptycki, "Against transnational organized crime," 134.

17 Senate Committee on the Judiciary (1969): Senate Report no. 91–617.

18 Gerard E. Lynch, "The crime of being a criminal," *Columbia Law Review* 87, no. 4 (1987): 661–764.
19 André Bossard, *Transnational Crime and Criminal Law*, 3.
20 Latter example from present author's own experience as a law enforcement official.
21 Bossard, *Transnational Crime and Criminal Law*, 5.
22 H. Richard Friman and Peter Andreas, "Introduction: International relations and illicit global economy," in *The Illicit Global Economy and State Power*, ed. H. Richard Friman and Peter Andreas (Lanham, Md.: Rowman and Littlefield, 1999), 5.
23 Peter Andreas and Ethan Nadelmann, *Policing the Globe: Criminalization and Crime Control in International Relations* (Oxford and New York: Oxford University Press, 2006), 255.
24 Present author's italics.

2 History and development of the concept of organized crime

1 A well known exponent of this concept (ethnic relationship, world conspiracy of organized crime, etc.) is Claire Sterling, for example in her books *Octopus: The Long Reach of the International Sicilian Mafia* (New York: W. W. Norton, 1990) and *Thieves' World: The Threat of the New Global Network of Organized Crime* (New York: Simon and Schuster, 1994). For a more nuanced view: Donald R. Liddick, *An Empirical, Theoretical, and Historical Overview of Organized Crime* (Lewiston, NY: Edwin Mellen Press, 1999), 5.
2 Jean Cartier-Bresson, Christelle Josselin, and Stefano Manacorda, *Les délinquances économiques et financières transnationales et globalisation: Analyse et mesure du phénomène* (Paris: IHESI, 2001), 17.
3 Peter Andreas and Ethan Nadelmann, *Policing the Globe: Criminalization and Crime Control in International Relations* (Oxford and New York: Oxford University Press, 2006), 17–22.
4 The Wickersham Commission, 1929–31, quoted in Dwight C. Smith, Jr., "Wickersham to Sutherland to Katzenbach: Evolving an 'official' definition for organized crime," *Crime, Law and Social Change* 16, no. 2 (1991): 135–54. The Commission was set up in 1929 by President Hoover.
5 Fred D. Pasley, *Al Capone: The Biography of a Self-Made Man*, 2nd ed. (London: Faber and Faber, 1966).
6 For a thorough discussion of organized crime paradigmata, see Boronia Halstead, "The use of models in the analysis of organized crime and development of policy," *Transnational Organized Crime* 4, no. 1 (1998): 1–24.
7 The most influential work was Leopoldo Franchetti and Sidney Sonnino, *La Sicilia* (Firenze, Italy: La Barbera, 1877).
8 Gerard E. Lynch, "The crime of being a criminal. Parts I and II," *Columbia Law Review* 87, no. 4 (1987): 664.
9 Michael Woodiwiss, "Transnational organised crime: The global reach of an American concept," in *Transnational Organised Crime,* ed. Adam Edwards and Peter Gill (London and New York: Routledge, 2003), 17–18.
10 "Upperworld" is a neologism coined as an easy shorthand denotation to balance the concept of "underworld." The term is often used to imply that its inhabitants are not that different from and often have a commercial relationship with the inhabitants of the underworld.

11 Stephen Mastrofski and Gary Potter, "Controlling organized crime: A critique of law enforcement policy," *Criminal Justice Policy Review* 2, no. 3 (1987): 271.

12 Matthew Brzezinsky, "Hillbangers," *New York Times*, 15 August 2004, section 6, 38.

13 H. H. Sing, "Ah Kong: The Singapore connection," *Police* 15, no. 2 (1983).

14 Convention Against Transnational Organised Crime (A/RES/55/25), Art. 2(a).

15 United Nations Office on Drugs and Crime, *Results of a Pilot Survey of Forty Selected Organised Criminal Groups in Sixteen Countries* (Vienna: United Nations Office on Drugs and Crime, September 2002), 2.

16 Margaret E. Beare, "Introduction," in *Critical Reflections on Transnational Organized Crime, Money Laundering, and Corruption*, ed. Margaret E. Beare (Toronto: Toronto University Press, 2003), xxiv.

17 Sam Porteous, *OC Impact Study Highlights* (Ottawa: Public Works and Government Services of Canada, 1998), 2.

18 www.fbi.gov/hq/cid/orgcrime/glossary.htm.

19 Thierry Cretin, *Mafias du monde: Organisations criminelles transnationales. Actualité et perspectives*, 3rd ed. (Paris: Presses Universitaires de France, 2002), 176.

20 H. Richard Friman and Peter Andreas, "Introduction: International relations and illicit global economy," in *The Illicit Global Economy and State Power*, ed. H. Richard Friman and Peter Andreas (Lanham, Md.: Rowman and Littlefield, 1999), 10.

21 Organization created in 1971, which represents some 260,000 Italian firms mostly in the commerce, tourism, and service sector, but also artisans; in general the companies are of small and medium size.

22 The price at which the counterfeit item is sold, not the price of the product it imitates.

23 Liddick, *An Empirical Theoretical, and Historical Overview of Organized Crime*, 3.

24 Leonardo Sciascia, *Il giorno della civetta* (1961) (Milan, Italy: Adelphi Edizioni, 1993), 54–55. English translation by Archibald Colquhoun and Arthur Oliver: Leonardo Sciascia, *The Day of the Owl* (Manchester: Carcanet Press, 1984), 51.

25 The expression "only suckers work" is first found in writing as being used by a bootlegger only identified as "Callano," *American Life Histories: Manuscripts from the Federal Writers' Project, 1936–1940.* The bootlegger in question was interviewed by Roaldus Richmond; the expression is from page 1 of the interview, which is deposited in the Federal Writers' Project, 1936–40, in the Library of Congress, Washington, D.C.

26 Alison Jamieson, "Le organizzazioni mafiose" in *La Criminalità. Storia d'Italia, Annali*, vol. 12, ed. Luciano Violante (Turin, Italy: Giulio Einaudi, 1997), 463.

27 Thierry Cretin, *Mafias du monde: Organisations criminelles transnationales. Actualité et perspectives*, 210.

28 World Bank, "$1,000,000,000,000 and counting: The cost of corruption," Press Release, 8 April 2004.

29 Vito Tanzi, "Corruption: Arm's length relationships and markets," in *The Economics of Organised Crime,* ed. Gianluca Fiorentini and Sam Pelzman (Cambridge: Cambridge University Press, 1995), 167.

30 David Kilgour, Canadian Secretary of State for Asia-Pacific, "La lutte collective des nations contre la corruption" ("Countries' common fight against corruption;" present author's translation), 3rd Global Forum on Fighting Corruption and Safeguarding Integrity, Seoul, Republic of South Korea, 29–31 May 2003.
31 Personal conversations over several years with (now Emeritus) Professor Ajit Singh, Queens' College, University of Cambridge.
32 Arvind K. Jain, "Models of corruption," in *Economics of Corruption*, ed. Arvind K. Jain (Boston, Mass.: Kluwer Academic Publishers, 1998), 13–34.
33 Vito Tanzi, "Corruption: Arm's length relationships and markets," 169.
34 Arvind K. Jain, "Corruption: An introduction," in *Economics of Corruption*, ed. Arvind K. Jain (Boston, Mass.: Kluwer Academic Publishers, 1998), 1–12.
35 Timothy J. Gilfoyle, *City of Eros: New York City, Prostitution, and the Commercialization of Vice 1790–1920* (New York: W. W. Norton, 1992).
36 This larger-than-life gangster-cum-politician has attracted the public's attention, from an early silent film *The Life of Big Tim Sullivan: Or, From Newsboy to Senator* (Gotham Film Co., 1914) to a recent book, Kevin Baker, *Dreamland* (New York: HarperCollins, 1999).
37 Gilfoyle, *City of Eros*, 252.
38 Ibid., 251–54.
39 Hell's Kitchen was another well-known slum on the West Side of Manhattan delimited by 34th and 59th Street, starting 100 feet west of 8th Avenue. Lumped together with Chelsea (i.e. until approximately 15th Street), the area is known as West Side and was the scene of Leonard Bernstein's musical *West Side Story* (1957).

3 The transnational crimes

1 Mark Duffield, "Globalization, transborder trade, and war economies," in *Greed and Grievance: Economic Agendas in Civil War*, ed. Mats Berdal and David M. Malone (Boulder, Colo.: Lynne Rienner, 2000), 76.
2 Neil Barnett, "Cigarette smuggling in Europe," *Jane's Intelligence Review*, 1 August 2005.
3 Robin Thomas Naylor, *Wages of Crime: Black Markets, Illegal Finance, and the Underworld Economy* (Ithaca, N.Y. and London: Cornell University Press, 2002), 11.
4 Peter Andreas and Ethan Nadelmann, *Policing the Globe: Criminalization and Crime Control in International Relations* (Oxford and New York: Oxford University Press, 2006), 17–22.
5 United Nations, *Global Illicit Drug Trends 1999* (New York: United Nations Office for Drug Control and Crime Prevention, 1999), 1.
6 My friend, Professor Arthur Gibson, drew my attention to this point in a series of personal encounters.
7 Release of the *2006 International Narcotics Control Strategy Report*, Foreign Press Briefing, Washington, D.C., 1 March 2006.
8 Joel Brinkley, "U.S. lists its pluses and minuses in fighting narcotics worldwide," *New York Times*, 2 March 2006, A13.
9 United Nations, *UN Chronicle*, special subject, xxxv, no. 2 (1998): 2–50.
10 United Nations, *UN Chronicle*, xxxiii, no. 1 (1996): 77.

11 United Nations, *Treaty Series*, vol. 520, no. 7515.
12 United Nations, *Treaty Series*, vol. 1019, no. 14956.
13 United Nations, *Treaty Series*, vol. 1582, no. 27627.
14 *National Drug Control Strategy: FY2009 Budget Summary* (Washington, D.C.: The White House, February 2008), 1.
15 www.drugsense.org
16 In fact, opium production in Afghanistan alone was 8,200 tons in 2007 and 7,700 tons in 2008. Most of the world's opium now originates from this country.
17 Rensselaer W. Lee, III, "Transnational organized crime: An overview," in *Transnational Crime in the Americas*, ed. Tom Farer (New York and London: Routledge, 1999), 3; White House, Office of National Drug Control Policy (ONDCP), *The National Drug Control Strategy, 1997. Budget Summary* (Washington, D.C.: ONDCP, 1997), 240.
18 Steve Hirsch, "Experts question global counternarcotics strategies," *Jane's Intelligence Review*, 1 November 2005.
19 Christina Jacqueline Johns, *Power, Ideology, and the War on Drugs: Nothing Succeeds Like Failure* (New York: Praeger, 1992), 174.
20 Chapter 11 in Max Weber, *Economy and Society* (New York: Bedminster Press, 1968), 956–1005 (a translation of his *Wirtschaft und Gesellschaft* from 1922).
21 Rensselaer W. Lee, III, "Transnational organized crime: An overview," 29.
22 Adam Edwards and Peter Gill, "Origins of the concept," in *Transnational Organised Crime*, ed. Adam Edwards and Peter Gill (London and New York: Routledge, 2003), 8.
23 Tom Farer, "Introduction," in *Transnational Crime in the Americas*, ed. Tom Farer (New York and London: Routledge, 1999), xv.
24 Council on Foreign Relations, *Rethinking International Drug Control* (Washington, D.C.: Council on Foreign Relations, 1997), 55.
25 As per July 2007, the prices on brand cigarettes were, very approximately, for one packet containing 20 cigarettes: in the United States, $5.00 (taxes paid); in the United Kingdom, £5.00 (taxes paid); "duty-free," $1.00. However, in the United States, there is a price differential between the various states: Virginia, $5.00; New York City, $7.50; Long Island, $4.60—which quite obviously constitutes an inducement to interstate smuggling of such product.
26 Campaign for Tobacco-Free Kids (30 April 2004); The British American Tobacco company, BAT, estimates that 30 percent of cigarettes and 70 percent of self-rolled cigarettes used in the United Kingdom have not been subjected to taxation, entailing a loss in government revenue of £2.6 billion. Neil Barnett, "Cigarette smuggling in Europe," *Jane's Intelligence Review*, 1 August 2005.
27 R. A. Radford, "The economic organization of a P.O.W. camp," *Economica* 12 (1945): 189–201.
28 Ian Black and Jan Martinson, "Tobacco firms sued over EU smuggling," *Guardian*, 7 November 2000.
29 Susan Wiltshire, Angus Bancroft, Amanda Amos, and Odette Parry, "'They're doing people a service': Qualitative study of smoking, smuggling, and social deprivation," *British Medical Journal* 323(7306) (2001): 203–7.
30 Source: Center for Public Integrity, *Tobacco Companies Linked to Criminal Organizations in Cigarette Smuggling—Cyprus and Middle East*. www.publicintegrity.org

31 Likewise, the counterfeiting of cutting-edge pharmaceutical products generates the same profits as the illicit traffic in narcotics, but the risk of apprehension is very low, and the possibility of receiving a custodial sentence, if apprehended, basically non-existent.

32 Barnett, "Cigarette smuggling in Europe."

33 Patrick Fleenor, "Cigarette taxes, black markets, and crime lessons from New York's 50-year losing battle," *Policy Analysis* 468 (6 February 2003): 14.

34 International Consortium of Investigative Journalists, *Tobacco Companies Linked to Criminal Organizations in Lucrative Cigarette Smuggling*, 3 March 2001. Report written by William Marsden documenting smuggling in China, North America, Italy, Latin America, Africa Cyprus and the United States. Reported by Maud S. Beelman, Bill Birnbauer, Duncan Campbell, William Marsden, Erik Schelzig and Leo Sisti.

35 "The BAT investigation: Paper trail to markets of the East," *Guardian*, 2 February 2000.

36 International Consortium of Investigative Journalists (2001), op. cit.

37 Barnett, "Cigarette smuggling in Europe."

38 OLAF is the French acronym: Office européen de lutte anti-fraude.

39 William Billingslea, "Illicit cigarette trafficking and the funding of terrorism," *The Police Chief* 71, no. 2 (2004).

40 Violation of 18 U.S.C.A §2339B, "Providing material support or resources to designated foreign terrorist organizations."

41 Fleenor, "Cigarette taxes, black markets, and crime lessons from New York's 50-year losing battle," 13.

42 Fleenor, ibid.; William Purdy and Lowell Bergman, "Unclear danger: Inside the Lackawanna terror case," *New York Times*, 12 November 2003.

43 See Edgar Allan Poe, "The purloined letter" (1844). The best way to hide something is to hide it in full view, where everybody can see it, but where it "belongs," namely among other items of the same kind.

44 Lynda Milito and Reg Potterton, *Mafia Wife: My Story of Love, Murder and Madness* (New York: HarperCollins, 2003), 124; see also Valeria Pizzini-Gambetta, "Review article: Mafia women in Brooklyn," *Global Crime* 8, no. 1 (2008): 80–93.

45 Subcommittee on Crime, Terrorism and Homeland Security of the Committee on the Judiciary, House of Representatives, 109th Congress, 11 May 2006; Karen Wutkowski, "US retailers want online sellers to fight theft," *Reuters*, 25 October 2007.

46 House Resolution 6491.

47 APACS, *Fraud: The Facts 2008* (London: APACS, 2008), 49–50.

48 Bob Sullivan, "Inside the stolen credit card market: Net chat rooms provide the perfect place for 'carders' to trade—outside the law's prying eyes," *MSNBC*, 2 February 2000.

49 *U.S. Attorney, Southern District of New York v. Ijmija Frjuckic*. Indictment 18 December 2003; U.S. Attorney, Southern District of New York, "Eastern European ATM operator and associate indicted by U.S. for multi-million-dollar ATM fraud," News Release, Department of Justice, 18 December 2003; Walt Bogdanish and Jenny Nordberg, "Stealing the code: Con men and cash machines; criminal focus on A.T.M.'s weak link," *New York Times Online*, 3 August 2003.

146 *Notes*

50 The violence exerted by organized crime has influenced many scholars in a less than helpful manner. Organized crime has no adequate conflict resolution mechanism and therefore has to resort to violence to resolve problems of territoriality and market share.

51 Roger Faligot, *La mafia chinoise en Europe* (Paris: Calmann-Lévy, 2001), 162–64; Alain Léauthier, "Cartes bleues made in Hongkong," *Libération*, 24 June 1992.

52 Moisés Naím, *Illicit* (New York: Doubleday, 2005), 99.

53 "Drawing lines in a dark place," *Economist*, 14 August 2008, 57.

54 Francis T. Miko, "Trafficking in women and children: The U.S. and international response," in *Trafficking in Women and Children: Current Issues and Developments*, ed. Anna M. Troubnikoff (New York: Nova Science Publishers, 2003), 1.

55 U.S. Public Law 106–386, Victims of Trafficking and Violence Protection Act of 2000, §102.b.8.

56 James O. Finchenauer and Jennifer Schrock, "Human trafficking: A growing criminal market in the U.S.," in *Trafficking in Women and Children: Current Issues and Developments*, ed. Anna M. Troubnikoff (New York: Nova Science Publishers, 2003), 32.

57 Adopted 15 November 2000 as Annexe II to United Nations General Assembly resolution A/RES/55/25.

58 The Fund was originally known as the United Nations International Children's Emergency Fund. The name was shortened to the United Nations Children's Fund, but the acronym UNICEF had by then become popular and remained in use.

59 The Swedish NGO Kvinna till Kvinna, quoted in D. Scharie Tavcer, *From Poverty to the Trafficking of Women for Sexual Exploitation: A Study of Casual Factors of Trafficked Women from Moldova* (Paper presented at the 5th European Feminist Research Conference, Lund, Sweden, 20–24 August 2003), 1.

60 Ethan B. Kapstein, "The new global slave trade," *Foreign Affairs* (November-December 2006), 105.

61 Rome Statute of the International Criminal Court, Article 7.

62 Ethan B. Kapstein, "The new global slave trade," 106.

63 Howard N. Snyder, "Sexual assault of young children as reported to law enforcement: Victim, incident, and offender characteristics" (Washington, D.C.: Bureau of Justice Statistics, U.S. Department of Justice, July 2000), 8, 10. The report is based on the FBI National Incident-Based Reporting System (NIBRS.) It should be noted that the NIBRS system, which is part of the U.S. Uniform Crime Reporting Program (UCR), is provided information from a limited number of participating law enforcement agencies. The latter cover approximately 10 percent of the U.S. population. Although the participating states are spread over the United States from Virginia to South Dakota and from Illinois to South Carolina, some scholars question if the data are statistically significant for the U.S. population as a whole.

64 Daniel S. Campagna and Donald L. Poffenberger, *The Sexual Trafficking in Children* (Dover, Mass.: Auburn House Publishing, 1988), 153.

65 The definition of child pornography accepted for use by Interpol is "the visual depiction of the sexual exploitation of a child, focussing on the child's sexual behaviour or genitals," Interpol Recommendations on Offences Against Minors, INTERPOL 61st General Assembly (1995).

66 Naylor, *Wages of Crime: Black Markets, Illegal Finance and the Under-world Economy*, 1–11.
67 A tropical hardwood tree that yields valuable timber. Native to Malaysia and Indonesia, *Gonystylus spp.*, occurring in peat swamps and freshwater swamp forest in Borneo, Sumatra, and Peninsular Malaysia, is the most valuable commercial tree species in Indonesia and fetches $368–710 /m^3 on the Malay market and $1,000/m^3 on the international markets once processed.
68 Adam Roberts and Will Travers, "CITES protects ramin: Indonesia scores big win in tropical timber conservation," *Animal Welfare Institute* (8 October 2004).
69 Merbau is the Malay name for a tropical hardwood tree. Like ramin (above), it yields valuable timber and is native to Malaysia and Indonesia. Of the several species, *Intsia palembanica* is of most concern in the present context.
70 Peter Andreas, "Smuggling wars: Law enforcement and law evasion in a changing world," in *Transnational Crime in the Americas*, ed. Tom Farer (New York and London: Routledge, 1999), 86.
71 Alice Blondel, "Dérive criminelle de l'économie du bois," *Le Monde diplomatique* (December 2003): 29.
72 www.trial-ch.org/trialwatch/profiles/en/legalprocedures/p289.html
73 This company—like the majority of all international tropical forest product companies—is incorporated in Malaysia and its main corporate officers are Malay nationals.
74 United Nations Security Council resolution 1343.
75 *Agence France Presse*, 21 March 2005.
76 *A more secure world: Our shared responsibility*, Report of the High-level Panel on Threats, Challenges and Change (UN Doc. A/59/565), 2 December 2004.
77 Pablo Fajnzylber, Daniel Lederman, and Norman Loayza, "Inequality and violent crime," *Journal of Law and Economics* 45, no. 1 (April 2002): 25.
78 Source: Istat (Italian National Statistics Office).
79 Maria Laura Iacobone, "Triadi o non triadi? Il crimine cinese nel bel paese," *Limes*, no. 2 (2005): 207.
80 Angelo Camuso and Emiliano Fittipaldi, "Mafia gialla," *L'Espresso* 54, no. 23 (2008): 31.
81 1,000,000 cigarettes with packaging weigh one ton.
82 Videocomunicazioni New Agency: www.videocomunicazioni.com/2008/05/marlboro-contrafatte-cinesi-sequestrate-a-napoli
83 Angelo Camuso and Emiliano Fittipaldi, "Mafia gialla," 32.
84 Alessio Mannucci, *Ecomafia 2007*. www.amadeux.it/forum/topic.asp?TOPIC_ID = 7197
85 Roberto Saviano, *Gomorrah* (London: Macmillan, 2007), 282–301 and the film produced from the book, Matteo Garrone, *Gomorrah* (Italy, 2008).
86 Italian Customs Agency (Agenzia delle Dogane), Press Release, protocol no. 3885, 11 July 2006.
87 Alessio Mannucci, *Ecomafia 2007*.
88 Angelo Camuso and Emiliano Fittipaldi, "Mafia gialla," 35.
89 "La mafia gialla controlla i clandestini. Per la prima volta in Toscana processato il boss della famiglia Hsiang," *La Repubblica—Sezione Toscana*, 18 May 1999, 1.

90 Bertil Lintner, "Chinese organised crime," *Global Crime* 6, no. 1 (2004): 84–96.

91 Sources: Derived from the author's meetings with case investigators, 13 March 2007 and 12 June 2007, in Washington, D.C. Matt Stiles, "Assassination plot part of theft ring case," *Dallas Morning News*, 4 February 2005; ICE (U.S. Immigration and Customs Enforcement, part of the Homeland Security Department) News Release, "Leader of organized infant formula theft ring sentenced to 14 years in federal prison," (Dallas, Texas, 2 February 2005).

92 ICE News Release, 2 February 2005, 1.

93 Conversation with Detective Scott Campbell, Fort Worth Police Department, in Fort Worth, Texas, 19 June 2007.

94 The vast majority of these are Palestinians or Jordanians. However, it should be emphatically noted that not all persons of Middle Eastern origin setting up convenience stores in low-income urban areas are involved in the kind of criminality considered here. The case investigators, with whom I discussed the issue, were eager to stress this point.

95 Jean-François Thony, "Money laundering and terrorism financing: An overview," Paper prepared for the IMF Seminar on Current Development in Monetary and Financial Law (Washington, D.C., 10 May 2000), 5. The acronym GIA is from the group's French name, *Groupe islamique armé*.

96 Beth Musgrave, "Grocers agree to plea deal," *Lexington Herald*, 31 August 2007, B1, U.S. Department of Justice (2007), U.S. Federal News Service, 1 May 2006.

97 U.S. District Court, Louisville, Kentucky, 31 May 2007, Action no. 3:03CR-116-C.

98 Tomasi di Lampedusa, *Il Gattopardo* (Milan: Feltrinelli, 1994), 41. (Present author's translation.)

4 Transnational crime and terrorism

1 For this chapter in general, reference is made to Peter Romaniuk, *Multinational Cooperation against Terrorism* (London and New York: Routledge, forthcoming), in the same series as the present work, Routledge Global Institutions.

2 Council of Europe. The Committee of Ministers of the Council of Europe adopted the Convention on 10 November 1976. It was opened for signature and ratification by member states of the Council of Europe on 27 January 1977.

3 I have elaborated this definition at least in part in objection to the wide politicization of the subject by diplomats and scholars alike.

4 John L. Austin, *How to Do Things with Words* (Oxford: Clarendon Press, 1975).

5 Baroness Nora O'Neill, "Speech and terror," paper presented at the F Club, Queens' College, University of Cambridge, 14 February 2005.

6 al-Jabha al-Shabiyah li-Tahrir Filastin.

7 Sebastyen Gorka, "The new threat of organised crime and terrorism," *Jane's Terrorism and Security Monitor*, June 2000.

8 Gorka, "The new threat of organised crime and terrorism." Anonymous former IRA member in conversation with present author.

9 Tamara Makarenko, "The crime-terror continuum: Tracing the interplay between transnational organised crime and terrorism," *Global Crime* 6, no. 1 (2004): 129–45.
10 Makarenko, "The crime-terror continuum: Tracing the interplay between transnational organised crime and terrorism," 133.
11 Ibid., 135.
12 Ibid., 135. Chris Dishman, "Terrorism, crime, and transformation," *Studies in Conflict and Terrorism* 24, no. 1 (2001): 48.
13 Paul Wilkinson, *Terrorism Versus Democracy: The Liberal State Response* (London: Frank Cass, 2001), 72.
14 Ralf Mutschke, "The threat posed by organised crime, international drug trafficking and terrorism," written testimony to the General Secretariat Hearing of the Committee on the Judiciary Subcommittee on Crime, 13 December 2000.
15 Louise I. Shelley, John T. Picarelli, Allison Irby, Douglas M. Hart, Patricia A. Craig-Hart, Phil Williams, Steven Simon, Nabi Abdullaev, Bartosz Stanislawski, and Laura Covill, *Methods and Motives: Exploring Links between Transnational Organized Crime and International Terrorism*, 23 June 2005, Federal Fund Award 2003-IJ-CX-1019, National Institute of Justice, Office of Justice Programs, U.S. Department of Justice.
16 Shelley et al., *Methods and Motives: Exploring Links between Transnational Organized Crime and International Terrorism*, 6.
17 Amartya Sen, *Identity and Violence: The Illusion of Destiny* (London: Allan Lane, 2006), 23–28.
18 Note that the Algerian *Groupe salafiste pour la predication et le combat* (GSPC) (Salafist Group for Preaching and Combat) has, among its main tenets, the exportation of Jihad.
19 Eric Pelletier, Jean-Marie Pontaut, and Romain Rosso, "Les Braqueurs du djihad," *L'Express* (22 December 2005) "Jihad's Armed Robbers" (translation by author).
20 Emmanuela Mylonaki, "The manipulation of organised crime by terrorists: Legal and factual perspectives," *International Criminal Law Review* 2, no. 3 (2002): 227.
21 Louise I. Shelley, "Identifying, counting and categorizing transnational organized crime," *Transnational Organized Crime* 5, no. 1 (1999): 1–18.
22 U.S.C. 2625 f(d)(2).
23 Mica Rosenberg and Miguel Angel Gutierrez, "Mexico's president says 'enough' to drug hitmen," *Reuters* (9 May 2008); Sean McCormack, "U.S. stands with Mexico in fight against organized crime," U.S. State Department Press Release (12 May 2008).
24 "Mexico police chief quits after drug gang threats," *Reuters* (18 May 2008).
25 I have retained the by now traditional denomination of Latin and South American narcotics trafficking organizations as "cartels," although this use, strictly speaking, is unhelpful since "cartel" refers to "an association of manufacturers or suppliers with the purpose of maintaining prices at a high level and restricting competition" (*The New Oxford Dictionary of English*).
26 *Jane's Intelligence Digest*, 1 February 2008.
27 Steven W. Casteel, Statement before the Senate Committee on the Judiciary, "Narco-terrorism: International drug trafficking and terrorism: A dangerous mix" (20 May 2003).

28 Statements by former Sicilian local boss Nino Giuffrè, *Il Siciliano*, 22 October 2003. See also: Salvo Palazzolo, "Trapani, fra Mafia e servizi deviati," *Limes* 2005, no. 2 (2005): 101–10.
29 Michael P. Arena, "Hizballah's global criminal operations," *Global Crime* 7, no. 3–4 (2006): 455–56.
30 "Foreign Terrorist Organizations (FTOs)," Fact Sheet, Office of Counterterrorism, U.S. State Department, Washington, D.C., 11 October 2005.
31 U.S. General Accounting Office, *Terrorist Financing: U.S. Agencies Should More Systematically Access the Use of Alternative Finance Mechanisms* (Washington, D.C.: GAO), 12 December 2003.
32 Steven W. Casteel, Statement before the Senate Committee on the Judiciary, "Narco-terrorism: International drug trafficking and terrorism—A dangerous mix" (20 May 2003): 1.
33 Karl Lallerstedt and Francesco Marelli, "Organised crime and international terrorism: Dancing together," *Institute Journal* 1 (2003).
34 Michael "Bommi" Baumann, *Wie alles anfing*, Preface by Heinrich Böll (Munich: Rotbuch Verlag, 2001): 128.
35 Kshitij Prabha, "Terror enterprise: Organisation, infrastructure and resources," *Strategic Analysis: A Monthly Journal of the IDSA* 25, no. 9 (2001): 1045–57.
36 Raymond K. Noble, "The links between intellectual property crime and terrorist financing." Testimony before the U.S. House Committee on International Relations, 108th Congress, 16 July 2003.
37 Formed by the borders of Paraguay, Argentina, and Brazil.
38 For a more elaborate five concentric circles concept: Michael German, "Squaring the error" in *Law vs. War: Competing Approaches to Fighting Terrorism*, ed. Shawn Boyne, Michael German, and Paul R. Pillar (Carlisle, Pa.: Strategic Studies Institute, U.S. Army War College, 2005), 12.
39 RAND-St. Andrews Chronology of International Terrorism.
40 Siobhan O'Neil, *Terrorist Precursor Crimes: Issues and Options for Congress* (Washington, D.C.: Congressional Research Service, 24 May 2007), 6; U.S. State Department, "Fact sheet: Foreign Terrorist Organizations" (Washington, D.C.: U.S. State Department, 11 October 2005).
41 Christophe Dubois, "Terrorisme. Quand le banditisme finance les islamistes," *Le Parisien*, 8 October 2002.
42 Source: Mr. Fred Walsh, U.S. Homeland Security Department, formerly ICE, 14 March 2007. Meeting in his offices in Washington, D.C.
43 For the sake of full disclosure, the present author admits to being that hapless official.
44 "Irish Republican Army (IRA)," *Encyclopaedia Britannica*, from *Encyclopaedia Britannica 2007 Ultimate Reference Suite* (2008).

5 The economics of transnational organized crime

1 George Vold, *Theoretical Criminology* (New York: Oxford University Press, 1958), 159–60.
2 Loretta Napoleoni, "Money and terrorism," *Strategic Insights* 3, no. 4 (2004): 1–4. Loretta Napoleoni, *Modern Jihad: Tracing the Dollars Behind the Terror Networks* (New York: Pluto, 2003).
3 Milivoye Panić, *Globalization and National Economic Welfare* (Basingstoke, U.K.: Palgrave Macmillan, 2003), 3.

4 Robin Thomas Naylor, *Wages of Crime: Black Markets, Illegal Finance, and the Underworld Economy* (Ithaca, N.Y.: Cornell University Press, 2002), 5.

5 Napoleoni, "Money and terrorism."

6 Robert Reiner, "Political economy," in the *Oxford Handbook on Criminology, 4th Edition*, ed. Mike Maguire, Rod Morgan, and Robert Reiner (Oxford and New York: Oxford University Press, 2007), 341–80.

7 Claudio Besozzi, Stefan Bauhofer, Nicolas Queloz, and Eva Wyss, *Criminalité économique* (Zurich, Switzerland: Edition Rüegger, 1997).

8 Guilhem Fabre, *Les prospérités du crime* (La Tour d'Aigues, France: Les Editions de l'Aube, 1999), 158–62.

9 Jean Ziegler, *Les seigneurs du crime. Les nouvelles mafias contre la démocratie* (Paris: Seuil, 1998).

10 Louise Shelley, "Transnational organized crime: The new authoritarianism," in *The Illicit Global Economy and State Power*, ed. H. Richard Friman and Peter Andreas (Lanham, Md.: Rowman and Littlefield, 1999), 25–51.

11 David Nelken, "The globalization of crime and criminal justice: Prospects and problems," in *Law and Opinion at the End of the Twentieth Century*, ed. Michael D. A. Freeman and A. D. Lewis (Oxford and New York: Oxford University Press, 1997), 251–79.

12 Maria Luisa Cesoni, "L'économie mafieuse en Italie: A la recherché d'un paradigme," *Déviance et Société* 19, no. 1 (1995): 51–83.

13 Anthony Giddens, *Modernisation and Self-Identity* (Oxford: Polity Press, 1991), 15.

14 The key publication remains Becker's Nobel Lecture from December 1992: Gary S. Becker, "The economic way of looking at behaviour," *Journal of Political Economy* 101, no. 3 (1993): 385–409.

15 Mark Findlay, *The Globalisation of Crime* (Cambridge: Cambridge University Press, 1999), 138.

16 Napoleoni, "Money and terrorism;" Raymond W. Baker, *Money Laundering and Capital Flight: The Impact on Private Banking*. Testimony before the Permanent Subcommittee on Investigations, U.S. Senate Committee on Government Affairs (10 November 1999); James K. Boyce, "The revolving door. External debt and capital flight: The case of the Philippines," *World Development* 20, no. 2 (1993): 335–49.

17 Kimberly L. Thachuk, "Terrorism's financial lifeline: Can it be severed?" *Strategic Forum* 191 (Washington, D.C.: Institute for National Defense Studies, May 2002): 1–7.

18 Calculation done by Napoleoni herself, "Money and terrorism."

19 Raymond W. Baker, *Capitalism's Achilles Heel: Dirty Money. How to Renew the Free Market System* (Hoboken, N.J.: John Wiley, 2005); Baker, *Money Laundering and Capital Flight: The Impact on Private Banking*.

20 Napoleoni, "Money and terrorism." Author's emphasis.

21 Racketeer Influenced and Criminal Organizations statute, 1970, 18 U.S.C. A. §1961 et seq. The act is analyzed in Gerard E. Lynch, "The crime of being a criminal. Parts I and II," *Columbia Law Review* 87 (1987): 661–764.

22 Richard D. Porter and Ruth A. Judson, "The location of U.S. currency. How much is abroad?" *Federal Reserve Bulletin* (October 1996): 883.

23 Brian M. Doyle, "Here, dollars, dollars … : Estimating currency demand and international currency substitution," International Finance Discussion

Paper no. 657 (Washington, D.C.: Board of Governors of the Federal Reserve System, 2000).

24 Theodore E. Allison and Rosanna S. Pianalto, "The issuance of series-1996 $100 Federal Reserve notes: Goals, strategy and likely results," *Federal Reserve Bulletin* (July 1997).

25 University of Michigan Survey Research Center, quoted in Porter and Judson, "The location of U.S. currency. How much is abroad?" 887.

26 Bank for International Settlements, Committee on Payment and Settlement, *Payment Systems in Eleven Developed Countries* (April 1989), supplemented by statistical updates: "Statistics on payments systems in eleven countries, figures for end-1988" (December 1989); "Statistics on payments systems in eleven countries, figures for end-1989" (December 1990); "Statistics on payments systems in eleven countries, figures for 1990" (December 1991); "Statistics on payments systems in eleven countries, figures for 1991" (December 1992) (Basel, Switzerland: Bank for International Settlements, 1989 et seq.).

27 "Debt hangover," *Economist*, 28 June 2007, 34.

28 Meeting with Mr. Jonathan I. Polk, Counsel and Vice President, Federal Reserve Bank of New York, at the bank's headquarters in Liberty Street, New York, on 8 March 2007.

29 Frederic S. Mishkin, *The Economics of Money, Banking and Financial Markets, 6th Ed.* (Boston, Mass.: Addison Wesley, 2003), 514. Mr. Jonathan I. Polk at above referenced interview.

30 U.S. Department of the Treasury, *The Use and Counterfeiting of United States Currency Abroad, Part 3* (Washington, D.C.: U.S. Department of the Treasury, September 2006), v.

31 Ibid., iv.

32 CMIR are submitted to the U.S. customs service on arrival and departure from the U.S.A. Reporting threshold is now $10,000 (until 1980: $5,000.) Cf. 31 U.S.C. 5316(a).

33 Porter and Judson, "The location of U.S. currency. How much is abroad?" 887.

34 The term is self-explanatory: Large amounts of notes are wrapped around the courier's body under the clothing in order to avoid detection by officials at border crossings.

35 The Federal Reserve System consists of the Board and twelve regional Federal Reserve Banks. Each Federal Reserve Bank has one or more Cash Offices (FRCO); there are in total 37 FRCOs.

36 For the shipments proxy method: Richard G. Anderson and Robert G. Rasche, *The Domestic Adjusted Monetary Base*, The Federal Reserve Bank of St. Louis Working Papers 2000–2002A (St. Louis, Mo.: Federal Reserve Bank, 2000); Edgar L. Feige, "The underground economy and the currency enigma," in "Public Finance and Irregular Activities," *Public Finance* (Supplement) 49 (1994), ed. Werner W. Pommerehne: 119–36; Edgar L. Feige, "Overseas holdings of U.S. currency and the underground economy," in *Exploring the Underground Economy*, ed. Susan Pozo (Kalamazoo, Mich.: W. E. Upjohn Institute for Employment Research, 1996), 5–62.

37 Anderson and Rasche, *The Domestic Adjusted Monetary Base*, 6.

38 U.S. Department of the Treasury, *The Use and Counterfeiting of United States Currency Abroad, Part 3*, ii.

39 Porter and Judson, "The location of U.S. currency. How much is abroad?"

40 Anderson and Rasche, op. cit.
41 Porter and Judson, "The location of U.S. currency. How much is abroad?" 886.
42 Feige, "Overseas holdings of U.S. currency and the underground economy."
43 *United States v. Eddie Antar* 53 F.3d 568, C.A. 3 (N.J.), 1995, 12 April 1995. The case study is a summary of and comments on Westlaw's KeyCite resume of the appeal to the 3rd Circuit.
44 *Herald Tribune*, 2 August 1983; IMF, *World Economic Conditions* (Washington, D.C.: IMF, 1984).
45 Jaime Marquez and Lisa Workman, "Modeling the IMF's statistical discrepancy in the global current account" (unpublished, Washington, D.C.: Federal Reserve Board, July 2000), see also: IMF, *Report on the World Current Account Discrepancy* (Washington, D.C.: IMF, 1987).

6 Initiatives against transnational organized crime

1 Quoted in Mathieu Deflem, *Policing World Society: Historical Foundation of International Police Cooperation*, Clarendon Studies in Criminology (Oxford: Oxford University Press, 2002), 214.
2 Peter Andreas and Ethan Nadelmann, *Policing the Globe: Criminalization and Crime Control in International Relations* (Oxford and New York: Oxford University Press, 2006), 84.
3 *The Emperor of Austria v. Day and Kossuth* (1861), 3 D.F. & G 217, 253; Andreas and Nadelmann, *Policing the Globe: Criminalization and Crime Control in International Relations*, 89; Lawrence B. Evans, *Leading Cases on International Law*, 2nd ed. (Chicago: Callaghan and Cogg, 1922), 23ff.
4 James Cockayne and Daniel Pfister, *Peace Operations and Organised Crime* (Geneva, Switzerland: Geneva Centre for Security Policy (GCSP) and International Peace Institute (IPI), May 2008), being a report from the 6th Seminar of Peace Operations, "Peace Operations and Organised Crime," 29–30 November 2007, at the GCSP, Geneva, Switzerland.
5 Andreas and Nadelmann, *Policing the Globe: Criminalization and Crime Control in International Relations*, 4–5.
6 Andreas and Nadelmann, *Policing the Globe: Criminalization and Crime Control in International Relations*, 10.
7 Ethan Nadelmann, *Cops Across Borders: The Internationalization of U.S. Criminal Law Enforcement* (University Park, Pa.: Pennsylvania State University Press, 1993), 466.
8 Barry A. K. Rider, "Law: The war on terror and crime and the offshore centres: The 'new' perspective?" in *Global Financial Crime: Terrorism, Money Laundering and Offshore Centres*, ed. Donato Masciandaro (Aldershot: Ashgate, 2004), 61.
9 UN Security Council resolution 1540 (2004).
10 http://eurojust.europa.eu
11 www.coe.int/T/e/Com/about_coe
12 Estella Baker, "The legal regulation of transnational organised crime: Opportunities and limitations," in *Transnational Organised Crime: Perspectives on Global Security*, ed. Adam Edwards and Peter Gill (London and New York: Routledge, 2003), 185.
13 Interpol's web site: www.interpol.org; Isabelle Mandraud, "Interpol démasque le pédophile," *Le Monde* (14–15 October 2007), 17.

14 United Nations Convention Against Illicit Traffic in Narcotic Drugs and Psychotropic Substances. E/CONF.82/15 of 19 December 1988, *ILM* (1989) 497. The United Nations Conference for the Adoption of a Convention Against Illicit Traffic in Narcotic Drugs and Psychotropic Substances took place in Vienna, Austria, 25 November – 20 December 1988.

15 Art. 3, §1.b. i–ii.

16 Art. 5, §4(f).

17 Art. 5, §3.

18 Art. 3, §3.

19 Art. 3, §5. a–b.

20 Art. 6, §9.

21 Respectively art. 7 and art. 9, §1(a).

22 Based on author's Interpol HQ experience: a major Pakistani heroin importer (later convicted) received telephone calls originating from Pakistan in a number of continuously changing telephone booths near his residence in Denmark.

23 Robin Thomas Naylor, *Wages of Crime: Black Markets, Illegal Finance, and the Underworld Economy* (Ithaca, N.Y.: Cornell University Press, 2002), ix.

24 Donato Masciandaro, "Money laundering: The economics of regulation," *European Journal of Law and Economics* 7, no. 3 (1999): 225–26.

25 Loretta Napoleoni, "Money and terrorism," *Strategic Insights* 3, no. 4 (2004): 1–4; Loretta Napoleoni, *Modern Jihad: Tracing the Dollars Behind the Terror Networks* (New York: Pluto, 2003).

26 Rows 1–4 are not intersections, while row 10 in Table 6.1 (area 1 in Figure 6.1), $A \cap -B \cap -C$, is not context-relevant in the sense that they are not necessarily of law enforcement interest, since capital flight, including tax evasion, may not be a criminal offence in some jurisdictions.

27 "Money laundering: Through the wringer," *Economist*, 14 April 2001, 68.

28 Board of Governors of the Federal Reserve System, *Report to Congress in Accordance with Sections 356(c) of the Uniting and Strengthening America by Providing Appropriate Tools Required to Intercept and Obstruct Terrorism Act of 2001 (the Patriot Act)* (Washington, D.C.: Board of Governors of the Federal Reserve System, 31 December 2002), 7.

29 Pierre Kopp, *Délinquances économiques et financières transnationales* (Paris: Institut des Hautes Etudes de Sécurité Intérieure, 2002).

30 Wolfgang H. Reinicke, *Global Public Policy: Governing without Governments?* (Washington, D.C.: Brookings Institution Press, 1998), 135–37.

31 Michael Levi, "Money laundering and its regulation," *Annals of the American Academy of Political and Social Sciences* 582 (2002): 183, fn. 3.

32 For instance, some citizens may have concerns over some of the characteristics of modernism, namely, according to Anthony Giddens, developed state surveillance and militarized order: Anthony Giddens, *Modernisation and Self-Identity* (Oxford: Polity Press, 1991), 15. Maria Luisa Cesoni, "L'économie mafieuse en Italie: A la recherché d'un paradigme," *Déviance et société* 19, no. 1 (1995), 51–83.

33 "AMJUR CRIMLAW §331," *American Jurisprudence, Second Edition* (updated November 2007): under the entry "Forfeiture of property involved in criminal proceeding."

34 Updated 1994, Money Laundering Suppression Act, see in particular Annex 4.5. "Specified unlawful activity" is defined in 18 U.S.C.A. §1956(c)(7).

35 Edward Krauland and Stéphane Logonico, "The new counter-money laundering and anti-terrorist financing law," *International Law News* 31, no. 1 (2002): 1.

36 An *interbank account* is defined in Title I, §1351 of Public Law 99–170 of 27 October 1986, codified as 18 U.S.C. §984 (c)(2)(B).

37 An example of the extraterritorial reach of U.S. legislation.

38 The Secretary of the Treasury, *A Report to Congress in Accordance with §357 of the Uniting and Strengthening America by Providing Appropriate Tools Required to Intercept and Obstruct Terrorism Act of 2001 (the Patriot Act)* (Washington, D.C.: The U.S. Treasury, 26 April 2002), 5.

39 David Evans, "Dirty money, clean banks," *Bloomberg Markets Magazine* (February 2004), 42.

40 A former U.S. Senate investigator, quoted in Evans, "Dirty money, clean banks," 42.

41 Evans, "Dirty money, clean banks," 42.

42 *Robert M. Morgenthau v. Anibal Contreras.*

43 "Bank of America settles money laundering probe," *North County Gazette,* 27 September 2007.

44 Liesa L. Fried, "Banks rethink laundering regs," *The National Law Journal* 11, no. 5 (1999): B1.

45 Jonathan M. Winer and Trifin J. Roule, "Fighting terrorism finance," *Survival* 44, no. 3 (2002): 87; Transcript of allocution hearing pursuant to guilty plea of Lucy Edwards In the United States District Court for Southern District of New York, 16 February 2002.

46 Levi, "Money laundering and its regulation," 189.

47 Financial Action Task Force on Money Laundering, *The Forty Recommendations* (20 June 2003).

48 Ludovic François, Pascal Chaigneau, and Marc Chesney, eds, *Criminalité financière* (Paris: Presses Universitaires de France, 2002), 57.

49 Egmont web site.

50 David Cay Johnston, "Arabs seek regional groups to fight money laundering," *New York Times Online*, 2 July 2004.

51 Consists of Belarus, PRC, Kazakhstan, Kyrgyzstan, Russia, Tajikistan, Uzbekistan.

52 The Mutual Evaluation Report (MER) by EGC was issued on 14 June 2007.

53 Known as *The FATF 40 + 9 Recommendations.*

54 The list of criteria can be found in FATF, *Annual Review of Non-Cooperative Countries and Territories 2005–2006* Annex 1, "List of criteria for defining non-cooperative countries or territories" (Paris: FATF/OECD, 23 June 2006), 13.

55 "Money laundering: Through the wringer," *Economist*, 14 April 2001, 68.

56 Peter Reuter and Edwin M. Truman, *Chasing Dirty Money* (Washington, D.C.: Institute for International Economics, 2004), 93.

57 Reuter and Truman, *Chasing Dirty Money*, 95.

58 Reuter and Truman, *Chasing Dirty Money*, 101.

59 Naylor, *Wages of Crime: Black Markets, Illegal Finance, and the Underworld Economy*, 134.

60 U.S. Treasury, *National Money Laundering Strategy 2002* (Washington, D.C.: U.S. Department of the Treasury, 2002), 11.

61 It would not seem possible to determine the scope of money laundering in the world. The then director of the IMF, Michel Camdessus, in 1998 estimated that 2–5 percent of global GDP or $600 billion to $1.5 trillion was laundered. Michel Camdessus, *Speech to the Plenary Session of the Financial Action Task Force* (Paris, France, 10 February 1998); Senator Carl Levin (Hearing before the Permanent Subcommittee on Investigations of the Committee on Governmental Affairs, United States Senate, 106th Congress, 9–10 November 1999, page 4) estimates that one half of this comes to the United States.

62 Reuter and Truman, *Chasing Dirty Money*, 114.

63 Reuter and Truman, *Chasing Dirty Money*, 115.

64 Performance and Innovations Unit of the Cabinet Office, *Recovering the Proceeds of Crime* (London: Cabinet Office, 2000), 30, 32.

65 Alan Travis, "Agency which targeted criminals' assets to be axed," *Guardian*, 12 January 2007, 14.

66 Most of the information in this paragraph originates from a confidential document obtained from *Géopolitique*, a Paris-based intelligence research organization. The nine-page document contains a two-page inter-office memorandum dated 8 June 2000, from the Banking Supervision and Examination Department of the Central Bank of the United Arab Emirates to the Governor of the Bank, entitled "Accounts of Russian nationals at UAE branches of HSBC Bank Middle East—money laundering" (in the following, "Inter-Office Memorandum") by which the examiners submit a seven-page report (in the following, "Report") to H. E. the Governor of the Central Bank of the UAE. The Hong Kong and Shanghai Banking Corporation (HSBC) is a large international bank incorporated in the United Kingdom.

67 Sharjah is one of the smallest of the emirates making up the United Arab Emirates; Deira is an area in Dubai, one of the largest and, economically, the most important of the emirates.

68 "Inter-Office Memorandum," 2.

69 Throughout, AED (Arab Emirate Dinars) have been calculated at the exchange rate valid on 17 November 2007 of $1.00 = AED3.6685. It is realized that the exchange rate at the time of these events was somewhat different, but in this paragraph, the denomination in U.S. dollars is for illustrative purposes only.

70 "Report," 2.

71 Pol. Maj. Gen. Peeraphan Prempooti, Secretary-General, Anti-Money Laundering Board, "Foreword," in *Anti-Money Laundering Office, Thailand* (Bangkok, Thailand: AMLO, w/o year), 2.

72 Meeting, 20 June 2005, with Pol. Col. Yuthabool Dissamarn, Deputy Secretary-General, AMLO, in his offices in Bangkok, Thailand. Unless explicitly stated to contrary, the remaining part of this paragraph is based on information obtained during this meeting.

73 "B.E." means "Buddhist Era" and translates into A.D. by the subtraction of 543.

74 In this paragraph referred to as "the Act."

75 *Anti-Money Laundering Office, Thailand* (Bangkok, Thailand: AMLO, w/o year), 7.

76 All extracts from the Thai law Anti-Money Laundering Act of B.E. 2542 (1999) were translated from the Thai by Pol. Maj. Gen. Peeraphan Prempooti, Secretary-General of AMLO.

77 The Office of the Narcotics Control Board was established by the Royal Thai Government on 16 November 1976.

7 Critical issues and future trends

1 Jeffrey Robinson, *The Merger: The Conglomeration of International Organized Crime* (Woodstock, N.Y.: The Overlock Press, 2000), 9.
2 Influenced to a large degree by Gary S. Becker, "Nobel Lecture: The economic way of looking at behavior," *Journal of Political Economy* 101, no. 3 (1993): 385–409.
3 In particular the crucial insights of Vito Tanzi at the IMF.
4 Christopher Aaron, "In place of strife: War and peace in the Italian mafia," *Jane's Intelligence Review*, 1 October 2005.
5 Walter Lippmann, *The Phantom Public* (New Brunswick, N.J.: Transaction Publishers, 1993 (1st ed. 1925)).
6 Moisés Naím, "The five wars of globalization," *Foreign Policy* 134 (January-February 2003): 35.
7 For example at the Cambridge America Forum on RICO at St. Catherine's College, University of Cambridge, on 19 September 2004.
8 *Le Monde*, 31 January 2008, 4; "The gap between supply and demand," *Economist*, 9 October 2008.
9 Confesercenti, "Le mani della criminalità sulle imprese," XI Rapporto SOS Impresa-Confesercenti (Rome, Italy, SOS Impresa-Confesercenti, 11 November 2008).
10 Stephen Brown, "Mafia extorts €250m a day," *Guardian*, 12 November 2008, 23.
11 Ethan Nadelmann, "Think again: Drugs," *Foreign Policy* (September-October 2007).

8 Conclusion

1 Mike Maguire, Rod Morgan, and Robert Reiner, eds, *The Oxford Handbook of Criminology*, 4th ed. (Oxford: Oxford University Press, 2006), 9.
2 WHO Conference of the Parties to the WHO Framework Convention on Tobacco Control, second session, provisional agenda item 5.4.1, "Elaboration of a template for a protocol on illicit trade in tobacco product," A/FCTC/COP/2/9, 19 April 2007.
3 Richard Lambert, "International co-operation against drugs and crime: Are societies losing the war?" in *Current Issues in International Diplomacy and Foreign Policy, Vol. 1*, ed. Colin Jennings and Nicholas Hopkinson (London: The Stationery Office, 1999), 63.

Annotated bibliography

1 Lynda Melito and R. Potterton, *Mafia Wife: My Story of Love, Murder and Madness* (New York: HarperCollins: 2003), 126–27.
2 Timothy J. Gilfoyle, *City of Eros: New York City, Prostitution, and the Commercialization of Vice 1790–1920* (New York: W. W. Norton, 1992).

Annotated bibliography

The purpose of this short bibliographical essay is to point the interested reader to a few of the works which are of particular interest in
this area. To render the listing as helpful as possible, it includes entries
of books, journals, web sites, and the cinema.

Books

Peter Andreas and Ethan Nadelmann, *Policing the Globe: Criminalization and
    Crime Control in International Relations* (Oxford and New York: Oxford
    University Press, 2006). One of the many values of this book is its application
    of the principle of "looking backwards in order to look forwards," since it
    provides well documented historical analyses of the main themes treated from
    the origin of so-called prohibition regimes to the hesitant beginnings of coopera-
    tion between police forces from different countries. This one-volume exposition
    of international law enforcement cooperation is the best and most thoughtful
    available.
James Cockayne, *Transnational Organized Crime: Multinational Responses to a
    Rising Threat* (New York: International Peace Academy, April 2007). For a short,
    but wide-ranging and interesting introduction to the subject, Cockayne's
    book is commendable.
Cyrille Fijnaut and Letizia Paoli, eds, *Organised Crime in Europe: Concepts,
    Patterns and Control Policies in the European Union and Beyond* (Dordrecht,
    the Netherlands: Springer, 2004). Series: Studies of Organised Crime, vol. 4. The
    edited volume is divided into three parts: the history of organized crime,
    contemporary patterns of organized crime, and organized crime control policies.
    Among the more noteworthy chapters are Michael Levi, "The making of the
    United Kingdom's organised crime control policies" and Claudio Besozzi,
    "Illegal markets and organised crime in Switzerland: A critical assessment."
Timothy J. Gilfoyle, *City of Eros: New York City, Prostitution, and the Com-
    mercialization of Vice 1790–1920* (New York: W. W. Norton, 1992). A truly
    fascinating work examining the sex trade in Manhattan in the nineteenth
    century and the beginning of the twentieth century, as well as the interaction

between individuals involved in criminal enterprises, in particular brothel owners, and local politicians. It constitutes the best possible introduction to the rise of organized crime in New York, to the transnational nature of local crime already in the nineteenth century by international trafficking in women, to the creation and development of so-called machine politics, and to the beginning of gang "wars" between so-called "natives" (gang members born in the U.S.A., typically of English or Irish origin) and more recent criminal immigrants.

Peter Grabosky, Russell G. Smith, and Gillian Dempsey, *Electronic Theft: Unlawful Acquisition in Cyberspace* (Cambridge: Cambridge University Press, 2001). A well written, broad introduction to the subject.

Mike Maguire, Rod Morgan, and Robert Reiner, eds, *Oxford Handbook of Criminology*, 4th ed. (Oxford and New York: Oxford University Press, 2007). The handbook, which is now in its fourth edition, was first published in 1992 and remains an essential tool for anybody interested in Criminology. Among chapters of particular interest, one notes Michael Levi, "Organized crime and terrorism" and Keith Hayward and Jock Young, "Cultural criminology."

Sally S. Simpson, *Corporate Crime, Law, and Social Control* (Cambridge and New York: Cambridge University Press, 2002). After a brief overview of the historical development of the subject-matter and an interesting discussion of the definitional difficulties (corporate crime versus white-collar crime versus economic crime, etc.), Simpson provides a deep and balanced analysis of the problem of deterrence in corporate crime. Although her development of the various themes is intellectually very rigorous, the book has the added value of being highly readable.

UNODC, *World Drug Report* (Vienna, Austria: UNODC). This excellent, yearly report of trends, production, seizures, consumption, and prices in the illicit narcotics market is indispensable.

Journals

Global Crime (Routledge). From its inception until 2004, this journal was published under the name *Transnational Organized Crime*. It constitutes the major forum for discussion among transnational crime scholars.

Crime, Law and Social Change. This journal contains many high-quality articles in the area.

Useful web sites

www.interpol.int: Interpol's excellent web site.

www.mcnabbassociates.com/bilateralex.htm: Listing of US bilateral extradition treaties.

www.europol.europa.eu: Europol's web site.

www.coe.int: Council of Europe's very informative web site.

www.unodc.org: UNODC's very useful web site, including a full dataset of drug seizures.

www.egmontgroup.org: The Egmont group of FIUs.
www.apacs.org.uk; www.cardwatch.org.uk; www.cifas.org.uk. All three are of
  interest concerning credit card fraud.

The cinema: organized crime and (self) publicizing

Robbers and other outlaws have fascinated the public imagination and
have, as a consequence, been portrayed in the theatre, in literature,
and, in particular, in the cinema. Apart from so-called thriller or
detective stories, also more serious literature has explored the socio-
political and, indeed, socio-psychological aspects of the relationship
between the alleged outlaws and the alleged "normal" or at least
norm-establishing society. One thinks in particular of Friedrich Schil-
ler, *Die Raüber* (1781). It is therefore not surprising that the cinematographic art form has also portrayed crime and, indeed, transnational
crime. The last 20–30 years have produced an important crop of cinematographic representations of organized crime, albeit mostly of a
rather stereotyped nature, for example:

- *The Godfather I–III*, 1972, 1974, and 1990, the first of which was
  based on a novel by Mario Puzo.
- *La Piovra*. Italian television series, 1984–2001.
- *The Sopranos*. U.S. television series, 1999–2007.

However, in more recent times, there is a new twist in the tale: fiction
and reality have become cross-fertilizing and, concurrently, inter-
nationalized. For instance, young men in Naples, Italy, who attempt to
rise in the ranks of delinquency, very often wear sunglasses wedged in
the hair on top of the head. This fashion is believed to have originated
from an organized crime movie in which the main character wore his
sunglasses in this way. But there is also an opposite movement, that is,
not from the cinema to organized crime, but from organized crime to
the cinema. Thus, it is well reported that in the course of the production of the television series, *The Sopranos*, referred to above, Italo-
American organized crime figures took a keen interest in and tried to
influence the choice of sartorial apparel of the characters playing
"Mafiosi" in the series. A final example is provided by Lynda Melito,
the wife of a well known organized crime figure in the New York area.
In her memoirs, she notes that after the release of the first film in the
Godfather trilogy, *The Godfather I*, the men in her "family" started
embracing each other in a way normal in Italy, but which had not been
usual among Italo-American males in her environment until then.[1]

Below is a listing of some recent cinematographic creations of interest in the present context. This listing is not meant to be exhaustive; instead, each chosen film provides a visual, but obviously fictional representation of one or more aspects of transnational organized crime.

David Cronenberg, *Eastern Promises* (U.K., 2007). Apart from its dramatic qualities, this film deals with a number of issues of import to the student of organized crime. First, the implantation in London, England, of the so-called *vory v zakone* ("thieves in law"), Russian organized crime; second, the sexual abuse and forced prostitution of a minor; and, third, the thorny subject of the infiltration of a police official into a criminal organization overseas, albeit with the blessing of the host country.

Atmos Gitai, *Promised Land* (Israel, U.K., France, 2004). This disquieting, but important film shows the trafficking of women—from Eastern Europe and the Baltic countries to the Middle East—and their being "broken in" by mass rape, violence, and auctioning. It likewise poses the crucial question of the role or lack of role of "territoriality" in a globalized world.

Martin Scorsese, *Gangs of New York* (U.S.A., 2001). This cinematographic creation is based on the non-fiction work of the same title by Herbert Asbury (London and New York: A. A. Knopf, 1928). The dramatic time of the film is 1840–63; it depicts a quarter-century of organized crime in Manhattan, in particular in the infamous Five Points neighborhood, in which the sex trade involving very organized importation rings in particular from Europe and the corruption of the political system into so-called "machine politics" were the main issues. The film should ideally be seen in conjunction with the reading of Gilfoyle's examination of vice in New York in the nineteenth century.[2]

Francesco Rossi, *Mani sulla città* (Italy, 1963). Corruption in the construction industry in Naples, Italy. A cinematographic masterpiece.

Matteo Garrone, *Gomorrah* (Italy, 2008), based on Roberto Saviano's book *Gomorrah* (London: Macmillan, 2007), shows the grip of the Camorra on Naples and surrounding areas, including some international aspects, such as Colombian drug traffickers and the illegal trade in and disposal of waste.

Index

GLOBAL INSTITUTIONS SERIES

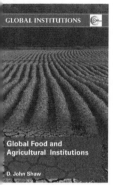

Routledge
Taylor & Francis Group

To order any of these titles
Call: +44 (0) 1235 400400
Email: book.orders@routledge.co.uk

For further information visit:
www.routledge.com/politics